*This Is Getting Old*

# This Is Getting Old

*Zen Thoughts on Aging*
*with Humor and Dignity*

Susan Moon

SHAMBHALA • *Boston & London* • 2010

Shambhala Publications, Inc.
Horticultural Hall
300 Massachusetts Avenue
Boston, Massachusetts 02115
www.shambhala.com

Some of the essays in this book, or earlier versions of them,
were previously published in the following places:
"Where Did I Put My Begging Bowl?" and "I Wasn't My Self"
(under the title "The Worst Zen Student That Ever Was") in *Inquiring Mind*,
"Stain on the Sky" in *The Sun*, "Leaving the Lotus Position" in *Tricycle*,
"House of Commons" in OnTheCommons.org, "Grandmother Mind"
and "The Secret Place" (under the title "If She Can Bear the Longing") in
*The Shambhala Sun*, "What If I Never Have Sex Again?" in *Persimmon Tree*,
"The Tomboy Returns" in *Jo's Boys*, edited by Christian McEwen, and
"Alone with Everyone" in *Turning Wheel*.

9  8  7  6  5  4  3  2  1

First edition
Printed in the United States of America

⊗This edition is printed on acid-free paper that meets
the American National Standards Institute Z39.48 Standard.
♻This book was printed on 30% postconsumer recycled paper.
For more information please visit www.shambhala.com.

Distributed in the United States by Random House, Inc.,
and in Canada by Random House of Canada Ltd

*Designed by Lora Zorian*

LIBRARY OF CONGRESS CATALOGING-IN-PUBLICATION DATA

Moon, Susan Ichi Su, 1942–
This is getting old: zen thoughts on aging with humor and dignity /
Susan Moon.—1st ed.
p.   cm.
ISBN 978-1-59030-776-2 (pbk.: alk. paper)
1. Older people—Religious life. 2. Aging—
Religious aspects—Zen Buddhism. I. Title.
BQ9286.7.O43M66 2010
294.3'440846—dc22
2010003821

*In memory of my mother, Alice,*
*and for my granddaughter, Paloma.*
*I never knew Alice when she was a child*
*and I will never know Paloma when she's an old woman,*
*but they both have inspired me with their enthusiasm for life.*

# Contents

# Contents

# Introduction

IN MY MID-SIXTIES AND IN GOOD HEALTH, I'm still a baby at being old. Now is a good time to investigate the matter and to develop courage, because getting old is hard. Getting old is scary.

I was never planning to get old myself. I was hoping to live through plenty more birthdays, but I wasn't planning on getting eroded in the process. Not long past sixty, as joints stiffened, as proper names fled, as hairs disappeared from some parts of my body and sprouted in others, I had to admit it was happening to me, too.

My Buddhist practice encourages me not to turn away from what's difficult. That's where the good news often hides, right in the middle of the mess. As a writer, too, the investigation of what's painful is what interests me the most. So I started writing about getting old. I wanted to look right into the face of oldness. What is it?

At first, I made a list of the difficult things that I was experiencing myself, like memory loss, sore knees, and fear of loneliness, and I set out to write an essay about each one. I wanted to teach myself how to get old without getting bitter. Then, as I kept on getting older, other things happened, both wonderful and painful. I became a grandmother, my mother died, and I kept on writing. Not only did I write about the things I didn't like that were happening to my body and my mind, I also wrote about how my relationships were changing because of age. As I wrote, I noticed mysterious changes, too, new openings into the spirit, new ways of being alive that aging was bringing me.

The book that emerged is personal, and I hope my concerns will connect with yours. I'm also thankful for those who write about the economic stresses of aging, the concerns about health care and housing, faced by so many older people.

Montaigne, in the sixteenth century, shocked the literary world by bringing his personal experience into his intellectual and philosophical writings. He said, "I am myself the matter of my book." He called his writings "essays," meaning *attempts*. I'm grateful to him for leading the way so long ago. These are my tries.

And this book is part of a larger conversation. I am in a generation of people who developed the habit of constantly talking to each other about what we are going through, and we are doing this together, too. I am not getting old alone, even when I'm alone in the house.

I'm part of a group in which five of us, all women over sixty, meet together to talk about our experience with aging, about what's happening to our hips and our family life. We call ourselves "crones," claiming the word. The dictionary says a crone is "a withered old woman." Some of us in the Crones Group are more withered than others, but we all have more withering to do before we die.

I'm reminded of another women's group I was part of back in the seventies—my "consciousness-raising" group. We met to take the veils away from the sexism that we had grown accustomed to and to help each other resist what was no longer acceptable to us. In the Crones Group, too, we support each other, but this time around we meet not to resist but to accept. I'm not talking about resignation, but: *This is how it is. This is what happens. How can we work with it?* And sometimes we find ourselves celebrating our age.

It annoys me when people say, "Even if you're old, you can still be young at heart!" in order to cheer up old people. Hiding inside this well-meaning phrase is a deep cultural assumption that old is bad and young is good. What's wrong with being old at heart, I'd like to know? "Old at heart"—doesn't it have a beautiful ring? Wouldn't you like to be loved by people whose hearts have practiced loving for a long time?

In the cluttered Berkeley office of the Gray Panthers group, the walls are covered with posters, portraits of faces of different ages, and under each photo are the words, "The best age to be is the age you are."

Old age is its own part of life. In thirteenth-century Japan, Zen Master Dogen wrote, "Do not think that the firewood is before and the ash is after. Firewood is a stage unto itself and ash is a stage unto itself." We are in the stage we are in; let's not think of ourselves as has-been young people, or as about-to-be-dead people.

But even the venerable Zen teacher Robert Aitken Roshi, in an interview about being old—he was in his eighties at the time—admitted with a laugh, "I often feel like a young person who has something wrong with me."

It takes a while for the self-image to catch up with the body. Glimpsing my reflection in a shop window, at first I don't think it's me, but someone much older than I am. When I went to my fiftieth grade-school reunion, I thought I had wandered into the wrong room: Who were all those codgers? And then the amazing recognition: in the white-haired old man's face, the boy who used to pull my braids at recess.

My mother, Alice Hayes, a serious poet with a fondness for doggerel, put it this way:

> In her old age, a rickety Ms.
> Took up learning the isness of is.
> Since it's not what one does,

She just WAS and she WAS . . .
Now she's gone off to BE in Cadiz.

Just so, Mom. As the Buddhist teacher Wes Nisker reminds us, we are called human beings, not human doings. Laotzu said it, too, long ago: "The way to do is to be." We older people, forced to slow down in the doing department, have a leg up on being.

My mother is one of two people who surprised me by making a disproportionate appearance in this book. She died just about the time I began to write about getting old, but she didn't let that stop her from showing up over and over in these essays. I shouldn't be surprised, since she's the old person I knew best. Something must have rubbed off on me as I watched her go from young old to old old.

The other person in my family who weaves herself repeatedly through the book is my granddaughter Paloma, born just before my mother died. She helps me understand old by showing me young. I see that we are different: I can't hang by my knees on the jungle gym, and she can't tell stories about life in the long-ago twentieth century. I see, too, that the years between us can be not a barrier but an enrichment of our pleasure in being alive together.

"Wabi-sabi" is a Japanese expression for the beauty of impermanence, the imperfection of things that are worn and frayed and chipped through use. Objects that are simple and rustic, like an earthenware tea bowl, and objects that show their age and use, like a wooden banister worn smooth by many hands, are beautiful.

I sew patches on my clothes and I glue broken plates back together. I love mended things. I like to take pictures of old things: the spiderweb of cracks in the windshield of a truck, bright mildew on the wall of an abandoned railroad station.

Teenagers pay good money for shortcuts to wabi-sabi when they buy designer jeans that are pre-faded, pre-frayed, and pre-ripped, but the true wabi-sabi look can't be made in a factory. It depends on the passage of time.

In *ikebana*—the Japanese art of flower arranging—flowers that wilt quickly are particularly valued because they demonstrate the beauty of impermanence. The very fact that they fade makes them precious.

I'm turning wabi-sabi. I study the back of my hand with interest: the blossoming brown spots, the blue veins becoming more prominent. With my other hand, I can slide the skin loosely over the bones. Can this be bad?

As I get older I am turning into myself. Job gone, children grown and living far away, parents dead. Can't backpack, can't do hip hop. Who am I, *really*? Now I get to find out.

# PART ONE

# Cracks in the Mind and Body

# Where Did I Put My Begging Bowl?

THE OTHER DAY, as I was filling out a form, I couldn't remember my social security number. I made a running start at it several times, but I couldn't get past 0-1-3. I had to look it up on last year's income tax form. To reassure myself, I recited the books of the Old Testament in order, without a pause. My great aunt paid me two dollars to learn them when I was ten, and they've stayed in my head for over fifty years. She said it would come in handy to know them by heart, and so it did, though not in the way she had expected.

Of course, memory loss is a normal part of aging. I bet Buddha sometimes forgot where he put his bowl down in his later years. But normal or not, it's inconvenient, even disabling. It hurts to forget what you used to remember. More than once I've had to enlist a friend to walk the streets with me, looking for where I parked my car. My mind, like my bladder, is shrinking with age so that it doesn't hold as much at once.

I now put people in my Rolodex by their first name if I think I'm going to forget their last. (This will only work as long as I can remember the alphabet.) Forgetfulness eats away at people's names starting at the end, so that sometimes I find myself clinging to the first letter of the first name like a person at sea hanging onto a splintered piece of the mast.

Last week I saw a man I know in the checkout line at the grocery store, a man whose name began, I felt sure, with P. Paul? Peter? My mother had a line for such a situation. "Hello! *I* can still remember *my* name! Can *you* remember *yours?*" But I prefer bluffing, so we chatted about paper versus plastic, and as I wheeled my cart away from the checkout stand I heard myself say, "Nice seeing you, Parker." It's a retrieval problem. Sometimes, if I stop worrying about it, the name walks casually out of the attic of my brain. "What's the big hurry?" the name says. "I was coming."

My mother went through a period of time when she said she couldn't remember ordinary words. She began writing them down—after she *did* remember them—in a little notebook that she carried around with her. *Catalog. Vascular. Pollen.* She thought she might be able to look them up when she needed them.

Now it happens to me, too: I know there's a good word for the thing I want to say and I can't get hold of it. If somebody else says it, I know what it means, but I can't seem to get it on the hook and reel it in, to put it in my . . . What do you call those wicker baskets that fishermen use?

And it's not just words, it's objects. Going through airport security at Midway Airport in Chicago, I was stopped because of some butter knives in my carry-on bag. (I don't generally travel with butter knives, but I was delivering these from one relative to another.) When the security officer decided I could take them on board, I heaved a sigh of relief and marched off to my gate, leaving my laptop behind in the gray plastic tray. I didn't realized what I'd done until the next morning, when I sat down at my desk to do my e-mail. After a few days of frenzied phone calls, I got the laptop mailed back to me. Now my name and contact information is on a sticker on the outside of the laptop.

When I had a particularly bad spate of memory problems last year, I got scared. For a couple of weeks, it seemed as though I forgot something serious every day, like leaving my purse in the shopping cart in the grocery store parking lot. (When I went back to the store an hour later, the cart was right where I'd left it, with my purse still in it.) I forgot simple things, too. I put a tea infuser into a cup and poured in the boiling water, but I forgot to put the tea leaves into the tea infuser first.

I went to see a psychologist about my cognitive functioning. He was over sixty himself, and first we reminisced about the sixties—*the* sixties, not *our* sixties—which helped to put me at my ease. Then he had me repeat strings of numbers and words, and he showed me a list of words printed in different colors of ink and had me name the colors as fast as I could. I did very well, he told me, "for my age." This was reassuring, though *for your age* has a sad ring to it, like, "You look good for a woman your age."

He told me to forget about the unimportant things that just clutter up the valuable space in my brain. And he said, "The best thing we can do for our brains at our age is to take a nap for half an hour every afternoon." It's a great idea; one of these days I'll make it a habit.

The visit helped me to accept that some memory loss is normal. It's what's happening. I used to think I was pretty smart, and now I am given the opportunity to let go of that identity. I have a different brain now, but as long as I'm grasping for the mind that I had twenty years ago, I suffer.

Then, too, there's the remembering. I may not remember the last names of lots of people I know, but I remember seeing my father standing in the doorway of our apartment in Chicago, looking like a stranger in his brown army uniform and hat, silhouetted against the light from outside. I must have been about two and a half, and he was going off to the war in the Pacific.

The older you are, the more of your life is in the past, the further back it goes, and the more historical your memories become. It's part of the job description of an older person to tell stories about the times that are gone—about what it's like to have your father disappear into a war, for example. Or about stepping off the Greyhound bus in Biloxi, Mississippi, forty-five years ago, to work on voter registration, and being greeted by the sheriff saying, "Now don't you be causing any trouble in our town, young lady." History's not what really happened—there's no such thing. It's what people remember and tell each other. But it's good if you don't go on too long.

One of my heroes is the late Studs Terkel, the great oral historian. It was important to him to get people to tell their stories, because, he said, "We live in the United States of Alzheimer's. People have forgotten their own history."

Sometimes I tell a story more than once, forgetting that I've told it before, especially when I'm talking to my children. I try to remember to say, "Stop me if I've already told you this," because I know from listening to my own mother how annoying it is to sit through a story you've heard before, pretending to be surprised at the punch line. Well, actually, it's only annoying if you remember the story, and this is one reason why old folks should hang out together. When I tell my old friend Bill a story for the second time, it doesn't matter because he's completely forgotten the story. This is called "beginner's mind."

Needless to say, I also remember terrible things, mistakes I made long ago. I remember throwing a wooden clog across the living room at a man I loved (and missing, fortunately). I remember crouching in the hall closet behind all the coats, with the door closed, so my children wouldn't hear me weeping.

Memory is plastic. What I remember isn't necessarily what happened, and how I remember it changes, depending on my changing focus of attention.

The body memories, like how you button a button, seem to be the last to go. A longtime dharma sister has advanced Alzheimer's and is no longer able to come to the Zen center to practice. But she did come, for a long time after she'd forgotten how to manage her life. Someone from the sangha would pick her up at home and bring her to morning *zazen* (Zen meditation). She didn't know where she was going or why, or who was helping her. She had to be guided from the car to the Zen center, and she had to be helped into her priest's robes. But once she was inside the *zendo* (meditation hall), the forms of her thirty-five years of practice were held in her body. I was moved to see how, during service, she was right on track, manifesting dignity and devotion. She recited the Heart Sutra from memory along with everyone else, she bowed when it was time to bow, and she exited the zendo when her turn came, greeting the abbot with a *gassho* on her way out. Outside the zendo she was lost again.

It's disturbing. Sometimes, driving along one of my familiar routes, I suddenly can't remember where I'm going. Then I'm in a dark place, even in broad daylight. I keep driving, slowly, hoping I'll remember where I'm going before I get there. So far I always have.

Zen Master Dogen, my favorite Zen master, wrote, "To study the Buddha way is to study the self. To study the self is to forget the self. To forget the self is to be actualized by myriad things." What does he mean by forgetting the self? Could forgetting my social security number or where I parked my car be steps in the right direction?

Once, twenty years ago, before I was "old," I had a strange experience. I woke in the middle of the night and I couldn't remember where I was. That wasn't the strange experience—it happens to most of us from time to time when we are traveling, as I was. But on this occasion, I couldn't remember who I was, either. The loud crack that had awakened me still rang in my ears; it might have been a door slamming in the wind, or a bowl breaking in my dream, but whatever it was, I fell through that crack into a dark space of not-knowing. I asked myself, "Where am I?" and then, shocked, "Who am I?" I lay in bed, waiting. For a frightening split second, I didn't know anything about who I was. I couldn't even have told you my name. Then my eyes grew used to the dark and I made out the window curtains. Ah! I recognized the room, in a family house by the sea, and everything, my whole impermanent life, fell into place. I wonder if that moment before the remembering is what it's like to have severe dementia. Or is this what Dogen was talking about?

7

If I lose my memory, will I stop being me, or is there a me beneath the memory? Is there a look in my eye that will stay no matter what I forget? The thing is, I don't have dementia now, so worrying about it is a distraction from being present in my life, taking good care of myself, and focusing my attention on what's important.

I believe that Dogen is talking about forgetting self-concern, and as I grow older, I notice what an excellent time it is to practice this kind of forgetting. It's all about letting go. I can forget about accomplishing all my ambitions—it's too late for that. I can forget about "making something of myself," a telling expression. Sometimes, for a moment, I taste the relief of letting this self fold gently into the next self, moment by moment, like eggs into batter.

It's time to forget some things and remember others. As a matter of fact, the planet needs all of us human beings to remember our history, and to remember our own accountability in it. History is a process that we keep on making out of the stories we tell each other about the past.

Before written language, or before most people had access to written language, people had only their own brains in which to store their knowledge, and so they were much more dependent on their memories than we are today and they gave their memories more exercise. Buddha's disciple Ananda, for example, had a particularly prodigious memory and recalled every single thing he heard Buddha say. He passed the teachings on after Buddha's death, and for centuries, the monks and nuns of the sangha recited the sutras to each other until they were finally written down.

The printing press made shared memory available to more people, and the Internet has further democratized our cultural memory. If you forget the books of the Old Testament, you can look them up. But there are still some things that the Internet can't remember for you, like where you parked the car. And the stories of your life—they aren't on the Internet either. How it was, for example, to be sitting in bed nursing your newborn baby when you learned on the TV news of Martin Luther King Jr.'s assassination.

Oh, by the way, it's *creel*, that wicker basket for fish.

# Stain on the Sky

WHEN MY FATHER was in his sixties, his retinas slipped their moorings. He told me he often dreamed of the colored world. In the dark of night, asleep, he could still see the blue water of Menemsha Pond and the white sails of his boat. But when he woke in the morning and opened his eyes, he was blind. He said that though these awakenings were painful, life would have been even worse if he hadn't been able to see in his dreams. He had lost the visual world—he didn't want to lose the memory of it, too.

Going blind is one of many things I try not to worry about as I get older. There's a genetic component to detached retina. It correlates with myopia (nearsightedness), and I am myopic, though less so than my father was. I started wearing glasses when I was twelve, and I remember my shock when the elm tree outside my bedroom window went from a Monet tree to an Ansel Adams tree. I had no idea such sharp focus was possible, and at first I didn't like it. Everything looked pointy. I could see the diseased spots on the leaves and a popped balloon caught in the branches.

Out of vanity, I wore my glasses only in the classroom and at the movies. Much later, after I got married, I wore them all the time. Then, after my divorce, I got contact lenses. Dates complimented me on the blueness of my eyes, but the contacts were a lot of trouble. They were uncomfortable and occasionally got stuck way up under my eyelids. They required at least as much daily care as a small pet—a canary or hamster—without providing any companionship. So I went back to the glasses.

But the contacts did come in handy when I was in residence as a monk for three months at a Zen monastery in California. Like all the monks, I had to take a turn on the crew that served our formal, silent meals. At breakfast, in the early-morning cold, I had to stand before the seated monks with a huge pot of steaming oatmeal and carefully spoon it into their bowls. The first person to be served was the abbot, an upright man who never suffered a lapse in attention. The first morning I served, I had my glasses on, and they immediately became so steamed up that I couldn't see what I was doing. I missed the abbot's bowl and served a spoonful of oatmeal right onto the mealboard in front of him. After that, I always rose ten minutes early on my serving days and put in my contacts.

After my father went blind, my siblings and I—his four adult children—were all told to get our retinas checked regularly. I went to an ophthalmologist, who shined an unbearably bright light into my eyes. I couldn't blink, because my eye was held open with a clamp. It was not painful in any ordinary way, and yet it *was* painful, to sit with my chin resting in the metal cup, unable to get away from the blinding light, unable to stop thinking of my newly blind father.

My retinas were fine. The ophthalmologist told me that if I experienced any unusual symptoms, like shadows falling across my vision, I should report it immediately.

One day I was studying a breakfast menu in a café, and all of a sudden I couldn't see it. There were big white holes in the daily specials, and ribbons of light, like the aurora borealis, played at the menu's edge. Worried, I called my doctor and described the symptoms. He said it sounded like a visual migraine, since it was the same in both eyes. If the symptoms didn't go away in half an hour, I was to call him back. They went away.

I have had several visual migraines since then, and I have learned to enjoy them, since they have never been followed by headaches. My favorite was the evening when bursts of colored lights danced across my field of vision, painting the face and black-robed body of a Zen teacher who was giving a talk in the dimly lit zendo.

I was about sixty when, on a Zen retreat in a remote village in Mexico, I had new and scary visual symptoms: I kept seeing nonexistent flocks of birds flying above the ocean. A dark ghost haunted the middle of my right eye, and a spark flashed at the bottom of my vision whenever I shifted my gaze. The retreat center's director made an appointment for me with an eye doctor she knew in a town two hours' drive away. She even hired a driver from the village and asked one of her employees, an aging beach bum from California who was fluent in Spanish, to go with me as my translator. I was embarrassed that it was such a major production, but it would have been worse than embarrassing to go home to California blind in my right eye. And so the three of us set off to the town of Tepic.

The eye doctor was a kind man, who said, through the beach bum, that he liked to meditate and was curious about Zen. In an ancient, dark office with high ceilings, he questioned me about my vision and typed my answers on a red manual typewriter. Then he examined my right eye and reassured me that my retina was not detached or torn—there was no emergency. He said he could see a spot at the bottom of the retina that he thought might be a certain parasite you get from pets that's common in Mexico—but I didn't have any pets. He suggested I have my vision checked when I got home. He wouldn't accept payment—he was doing this as a favor for his friend, the director of the retreat center—so I later sent him a Spanish-language book about Zen.

The symptoms all went away by themselves except for the shadow, which the California eye doctor told me was just a big "floater"—a tiny, harmless clump of cells within the vitreous humor, the clear gel filling the eye. After a while, he said, my brain would correct for it, and I wouldn't even see it anymore.

It didn't go away—in fact it got bigger—but I learned to see through it, or around it. I often think my glasses are dirty, which indeed they often are, but after I clean them, the gray spot is still there. I notice it when I look at a solid field of color, like the sky. Still, that stain on the sky is not just a blot in my vision; it's what's in front of me, a reminder to be grateful that I can see as well as I can.

In recent years I've fallen in love with taking photographs. The sun lays its light on whatever it meets, and I have only to raise my camera to my eye and put a frame around what's given to me. I've been taking pictures lately of screens, veils, curtains— things that seem to obstruct vision. But when I focus my camera on the veil itself, it becomes the subject. What's in the way is not in the way after all.

My father went blind one eye at a time. After the first retina detached, he continued with all his normal activities, even though he didn't have binocular vision. Five years later, the second retina detached, and he underwent a series of surgeries—five in all—in an attempt to save some part of his vision. The surgeon was a star doctor who had pioneered retinal surgery. He was passionately concerned with his patient's retinas, but not concerned with the person who was attached to the retinas. After the first surgery, my father had to sit up in bed for a week with his eye bandaged. He was allowed to rest his chin on a board, but that was it. All he wanted was to lie down. He developed such a bad headache that he thought he had a brain tumor. And after all that, when they took the bandage off, he still couldn't see.

At about that time I had a series of dreams in which my camera broke: I dropped it and the lens shattered; the shutter got stuck and wouldn't open; sand got into the gears, and I couldn't advance the film.

At last my father gave up and decided to go about the business of being blind. He went to a residential training program for newly blind adults, where he learned how to get around with a cane and how to read Braille.

After he went blind, my father had two more children with his young second wife—children he never saw. He became a familiar figure in his neighborhood, walking the children to nursery school with his white cane in one hand, his older child's hand in the other, the baby in the carrier on his back. Or he would walk their dog, Alfie, a rambunctious Siberian husky who was sometimes mistaken for a seeing-eye dog but was quite the opposite. Alfie pulled vigorously on his leash while my father stood at the curb, deciding with his ears when it was safe to cross.

When I was sixty-five, I had another bout of seeing non-existent flashing lights and imaginary flocks of birds, just as I had in Mexico, this time in my left eye. I was home in California, and I went immediately to the eye doctor, who told me the retina was thin but OK. He sent me home, saying the symptoms would probably go away, but if they didn't, or if anything changed, I was to let him know right away. If a little rupture developed, he said, he'd be able to tack the retina right back down in his office with a laser beam.

The imaginary birds and the flashing lights departed the next day, but the day after that I noticed a dark blot across the lower left corner of my visual field. This time it didn't drift across my eye like a floater. It was like the shadow that appears in the corner of a photo when your finger is obstructing the edge of the lens. Because it only covered a small part of the visual field, it didn't interfere with my vision in any practical way.

I noticed it with my body more than my mind. I drove to a Japanese restaurant for a lunch meeting with an acquaintance, and all during the meal I watched the shadow lift and shift like a curtain in a light breeze. I didn't mention it to my lunch companion, but while I was eating my sushi, it became clear to me that this was different, and I knew that the next thing I needed to do was go to the eye doctor. I seemed to see myself through the wrong end of a telescope, small and far away, eating a dragon roll. I was calm and afraid at the same time.

After lunch, my nephew, who was staying with me at the time, drove me to the eye doctor's office and then went to park the car.

"You have a detachment," the doctor said.

"Are you going to sew it back down, like you said?"

"It's too big for that," he said. "I can't do this one. You need to go right to surgery. You're lucky that the excellent Dr. Jones is still here. She can take you right now."

I called my nephew on his cell phone to tell him the news, but he didn't answer, so I left him a message saying, "It turns out I *do* have a retinal detachment and they have to do surgery." I must have been in shock, because I added, with an inappropriate casualness, "You don't need to wait. Go on home and I'll call you when I'm ready to be picked up."

The surgeon was an attractive blonde in a stylish blouse and skirt and high heels, whose office was down the hall. It was the end of the workday, and she had been about to go home, so she'd taken off her white coat. She looked stylish, not like an eye surgeon. No one was left in the ophthalmology clinic but the two of us. As I sat in her chair, there was a banging at the outer office door, now locked, and my nephew's voice calling me. "Sue, are you in there?"

The doctor let him into her office.

"I'm not going home!" he said. "If you have a detached retina, I think I should stay here with you."

He sat on a stool, a quiet comfort. The doctor explained that although I saw the shadow in the lower left corner of my eye, it was really in the upper right, at about ten o'clock, since the brain reverses everything we see. (We are actually standing upside down on the surface of the earth. How fortunate that the force of gravity is strong enough to keep us from falling into the sky!) She explained that it was as if a flap of wallpaper had come loose and lifted off the wall, and water had gotten in behind it. She was going to inject a gas bubble into my eye that would float upward, pressing the torn retina against the back of the eyeball where it belonged. The following day I would come back for the laser surgery.

When she stuck a needle through my lower lid to anesthetize my eyeball, I was glad Max was there. It wasn't so much the physical pain of the injection that bothered me as the idea of having a long needle stuck into my eyeball. I squeezed hard on the arms of the chair until she pulled the needle out again.

In a few minutes the anesthetic took effect, and I couldn't feel it when the doctor injected the gas bubble into my eye, but I saw it right away—not one big one, but several middle-sized silvery balloons and lots of little ones, bumping together like balls of mercury. She put a bandage over my eye and told me to come back the next day for the laser surgery.

Until the gas bubble dissipated, which would be in about a week, I had to keep my head cocked sideways, so that ten o'clock was at the top, and I couldn't lie down. That night I slept, or tried to sleep, in an armchair, with my head propped up on pillows.

Max took me back to the hospital the next day for the laser surgery. "Do you want him to come in with you?" asked the doctor.

"Yes please," I said.

This time there was no anesthesia, because you can't anesthetize against the light. Each stitch of the laser gun produced an explosion of light and a sudden ache inside my eye. The laser beam burns the tissue of the retina with its heat, and it is the scarring itself that binds the retina back to the wall of the eye. How odd that the eye, the organ of light, is healed with a beam of light.

The surgeon was kind and kept telling me how well I was doing. At one point I asked her for a rest, and she paused between stitches. The whole procedure took no more than ten minutes, but it was ten minutes with enough light for a decade.

I didn't need the eye patch anymore. I could see a little bit with my left eye, around the gas bubbles, and I could see fine out of my right eye, but I took Max's elbow anyway to walk back to the car. I was lucky to have his help. If he hadn't been staying with me at the time, I probably could have found a friend to take me, and failing that, I could have taken a cab. But the older you get, the more often you have to go to the doctor, and the more you want someone you love to take you there.

At night, I propped myself up in an armchair, my head to the side. By day, I walked around with my head tipped sideways, or sat at my desk with my head propped on my hand. I watched the gas bubbles merge into one big one with lots of tiny ones around the circumference, like a setting of precious stones in a ring. When I moved my head they rolled around at the bottom of my vision, like marbles in a bowl, though of course they were really rolling around at the top. Each day I was happy to see that they were smaller; when they were all gone I'd be able to hold my head up straight, and lie down to sleep at night.

I thought constantly of my father. As the days went by, I got a painful crick in my neck, and I didn't sleep much in my armchair, but it was nothing to what my father had gone through—and he had still ended up blind. I felt him cheering me on, urging me to keep my head bent to the side in spite of the cramp in my neck, urging me not to lie down at night no matter how tired I was, urging me to do whatever I could to save my sight. I knew he didn't want me to be blind. Sometimes, thinking of him, I pretended I was blind, and I felt my way around the house with my eyes closed. But the most ordinary activities were beyond me, like making a cup of tea, or putting on matching socks, or getting the toothpaste onto the toothbrush—all the things he had to learn to do over again when he went blind at age sixty. His courage in meeting his blindness was evident to me in a new way.

Each day the gas bubbles got smaller and I could see more of the rest of the world around them, and on the sixth day, they were gone. I drove myself to the doctor and she said that now I could uncrick my neck. All was well with my eye, and my retinal tear was healing. I've been able to see just fine since then, except in the dark, of course.

A couple of months after my retinal detachment, I was one of a group of writers and artists at a monthlong residency in the Adirondacks, in northern New York State. One November night a sudden blizzard enveloped us, accompanied by thunder and lightning and howling wind. "What about the chickens?" exclaimed one of the writers. "They'll freeze!" Several people grabbed flashlights and set out into the storm, and I tagged along. We walked a couple of hundred yards up the road to the vegetable garden, to catch the chickens and put them back into the chicken coop for the night, so they wouldn't perish in the unexpected snow. Some people shone the flashlights on the chickens, while others crawled on their bellies under the garden shed to catch the frightened birds. But I had neither a flashlight nor knees that allowed me to crouch down in the snow, and realizing I was useless, I started back to the house.

My feet could feel the smoothness of the road, and I could see the lights of the house through the trees. Every once in a while there was thunder and lightning. But after I'd been walking for a while, I noticed that the lights of the house weren't getting any closer, and I realized that my feet had found a road, yes, but the wrong road, the road that branched off to the tennis court.

I knew the right road was just a short distance away, on the other side of a little rise, and so I struck out through the trees, aiming straight for the lights of the house. It couldn't have been more than a hundred yards away. The snow was deep and my sneakers and jeans were immediately soaked. Then all of a sudden the lights of the house went out. The power had failed in the storm. There was nothing to aim for and no path under my feet. The wind was blowing and the snow was falling. I called out as loud as I could, "Hello! Can anybody hear me? Hello!" but my voice was thrown away by the wind. I walked slowly in what I thought was the direction of the house, putting my hands out in front of me to keep from walking into a tree. I might as well have been blind.

Then the ground suddenly dropped away in front of me and I slipped down an embankment and landed in the snow, striking my knee on a rock on the way down. I sat there for a minute, taking stock. I was all right. I would be able to get up and walk some more, but which direction? How stupid I had been, not wanting to miss the adventure of the chickens, and how cold. No hat, no gloves, and worst of all no flashlight. I imagined myself stumbling in circles in the dark, disoriented by the howl of the storm, stumbling and falling. No one would know to look for me, because they would all assume I was back in my room, asleep in my bed. Even the chickens were probably safe in their coop by now. I could freeze to death during the night, a stone's throw from the house.

I struggled to my feet, and just then there was another clap of thunder. The flash of lightning that followed showed me, just for an instant, the house, fifty yards away. Luckily I was facing the right direction to see it. And then it was gone again. I aimed through deep snow toward where it had been, testing each step before I put down my weight, and when I got a little closer I saw candlelight flickering in the windows. Having my retinas still attached made all the difference. I thought of my father, and I was grateful for the advances in ophthalmology that had come too late for him but not for me.

I remember when I saw my father blind for the first time. He was standing at the baggage claim in Boston's Logan Airport. I had flown in from California to visit him. My father's back was to me. He stood beside his wife, one arm through hers, the other holding a white cane. What got me was the way he held his head cocked, listening. It was the stance of a blind person, and I cried as I came up behind him. I had never seen my powerful and charismatic father standing like that before, waiting, just waiting.

During my visit, he kept asking anxiously what time it was, as if to orient himself in the days that now passed without any change in the length of the shadows. I went to the Boston Society for the Blind and bought him a Braille pocket watch—he had always used a pocket watch, fastened by a splice of rope to a belt loop. He cried when I gave it to him, and he kept it handy the rest of his life. After he died, his wife sent it to me. The white enamel of the face had been rubbed away by his thumb.

# Leaving the Lotus Position

I SIT IN A CHAIR. Yes, of course, but I mean I sit zazen in a chair. Zazen is Zen meditation, and in English we call it sitting, just sitting. Meditating in a chair is a recent development for me, arising no doubt from a karmic web of causes and conditions, but the primary one is osteoarthritis in my knees.

Everybody knows that a Zen student truly dedicated to the way sits cross-legged on the floor. Buddha was sitting cross-legged when he was enlightened under the pipal tree twenty-five hundred years ago, and there are millions of Buddha statues to prove it—sitting cross-legged on altars and bookshelves all over the world. Several of them are in my house.

The image of Buddha in seated meditation is the essential icon of Buddhism. And eight hundred years ago, Master Dogen, founder of Soto Zen in Japan, instructed seekers of the way to "sit either in the full-lotus or half-lotus position." These are ancient yogic *asanas*, sacred positions—they come with a warranty. Back in my limber days, I believed that I was bound to get enlightened if I just sat still long enough in half lotus on my black *zafu* (round meditation cushion). Now I see how unreasonable it would be if the cross-legged people were the only ones who got to cross over to the other shore.

These days sitting cross-legged causes me pain that is more than instructive. Everybody knows that not turning away from suffering is at the heart of Zen practice, and this includes not turning away from pain in the knees. *Sesshins* (long Zen meditation retreats) are an opportunity to learn to sit through pain. When there is pain in the knees, if I can see it as nothing other than pain in the knees, then I will be a happy person with pain in my knees. So I have been taught, during more than thirty years of Zen practice.

Some years ago, when I was still a floor sitter, a fellow practitioner had to move to a chair after knee surgery. (My anecdotal evidence suggests that a remarkably high proportion of Zen practitioners require knee surgery.) I asked how he liked it, and he said he missed his pain because now it was "harder to focus" during zazen. That threw me for a loop. I too have found that pain focuses the mind, but what does it focus the mind *on*? Pain! Is that useful?

Another friend had an epiphany in zazen. He was hurting, but he promised himself he wouldn't move before the end of the period, no matter what. The pain got worse and worse, and he just stayed still and stuck to his wall-gazing, and a few minutes before the end of the period, the whole universe opened and he saw that everything was everything. "No pain no gain," he explained, when he described the experience to me later. That never happened to me, though.

A teacher once told me, "If you avoid pain now, what will you do down the line when you are old and sick and have pain you can't avoid? Don't you want to learn to live with it?" I've decided to cross that bridge when I come to it. I figure there's enough pain coming my way anyway, why should I take on extra?

I *have* learned some things about pain through my sitting practice. If I move to adjust my posture prematurely, the pain will chase me wherever I go, but if I just sit still when the pain starts, it often goes away, or recedes into the background. That kind of pain is like a child who wants attention and gets bored if you don't respond. This anti-fidgeting training also has useful applications to secular life beyond the zendo, to the concert hall for example, or the business meeting, or the MRI gurney.

I have also learned that there comes a point in zazen when the pain is so intense that I know it's *not* going to ebb away—it just gets worse, until I am raging against it and against a spiritual practice that would ask this of me. Pain is, after all, an early warning system devised by evolution to prevent us from injuring ourselves. The reason it hurts when you touch the hot stove is so that you don't burn the skin off your hand.

Pain is an important aspect of ritual in various religious traditions: the *penitentes* beat their backs bloody during Holy Week; some pilgrims climb up stone steps on swollen knees to sacred shrines; Native Americans on vision quests stand still and naked in the sun's burning heat. But these are special rites of passage, not everyday practices.

I have come to the point of diminishing returns as far as sitting cross-legged goes. When I started practicing Zen, I was thirty-two and sat in a half-lotus position with manageable discomfort. My legs hurt in sesshin, but I knew this was part of the bargain. Now in my sixties I have arthritis in my knees. I can sit cross-legged for a little while if I make elaborate arrangements with several extra support cushions propping me up, but after about fifteen minutes the pain begins in earnest anyway. When I consulted an orthopedist last year about the trouble I was having with my knees, I mentioned that I do Zen meditation and he scolded me for sitting cross-legged. I now have doctor's orders to sit in a chair. I could have asked him for a note for my teacher, but I didn't need to, because these days, fortunately, all the Zen teachers I know have become tolerant of chair-sitting. It's allowed, even though it's not exactly de rigueur. The harsh taskmaster within is the one who still gives me trouble.

So it was a turning point when I swallowed my pride and sat my first sesshin in a chair. There were several other chair-sitters, and I was grateful not to be alone at this higher elevation, not to have my lone head sticking up like a sore thumb in the thin air above the clouds. Lo and behold, this was the first sesshin in years in which I wasn't fighting myself—*Why the hell am I doing this?* I settled down. It was the first sesshin in which I didn't once pray for the bell to hurry up and ring for the end of the period. I was able to be here now—or rather, at this writing, to be there then.

I praise the chair as a spiritual aid. A chair is a tool for sitting in, a gift invented and produced by human beings for human beings. This body knows how to sit in a chair. There's a lovely geometry to a person in a chair, with the legs, seat, and back of the living body parallel to the legs, seat, and back of the chair, in a double zigzag, expressing the rightness of right angles.

Sometimes I miss being down on the floor—it feels good to be grounded, to *get down*. So I remind myself: if I am sitting on a chair and the chair is on the floor, then I am sitting on the floor. Besides, it's important to be able to get up again when the bell rings. There are two parts of Zen practice: sitting down and getting up, and for me, getting up from the floor takes too much time away from the next activity. I don't want to miss my chance to use the bathroom before the next period of zazen.

In a recent sesshin at a traditional Zen practice center, my second in a chair, I was the only chair-sitter, even though I wasn't the oldest person. This gave me pause. Was I the only one because I was the person with the least amount of cartilage in my knees, or because I was the wimpiest person, or the person who cared the least what others thought of me? I realized, sitting there in my chair, that it didn't matter. The only real question was and always is: am I making my best effort? If I am making my best effort while sitting in a chair, then I am sitting perfectly.

There are plenty of challenges to chair-sitting, so don't worry that it's too easy—you can still be miserable. The five hindrances of lust, sloth, ill will, restlessness, and doubt assault me in a chair as easily as they did when I sat on the floor. Pain visits me, too, on occasion, sharp and hot between the shoulder blades, but I know it's not injuring me, and it doesn't stay.

Sitting in a chair, I feel gratitude for the practice. I enjoy sitting upright. I enjoy my breathing. I am not guarding against the onset of pain and I am not fighting with myself for being a sissy. I am not making bargains with myself the whole time, such as: *ten more breaths and then I will allow myself to move.* I check my posture: I feel my feet firmly planted on the floor, I feel the uprightness of my spine, I feel my sitting bones on the seat of the chair. I am close to the others in the room; whether they are on the floor or in chairs, we are practicing together, held by the same silence.

What's next? Perhaps I'll go on to hammock practice, or sitting zazen in a chaise longue, poolside. I'll let you know how that goes when I get there.

# The Breathing Tube

*On a Sunday afternoon in late September, my eighty-four-year-old mother, Alice, went out for a drive with an elderly man she jokingly called her "boyfriend," who took her places after she gave up driving. Going north on Chicago's Outer Drive, they came over a rise and crashed into a stalled car in the middle of the road.*

## THE FIRST WEEK

MY MOTHER'S SWOLLEN HANDS stayed where they lay by her sides when I leaned down to kiss her at the hospital. Her breath smelled rotten. Worst of all was the breathing tube they had plunged down her throat, a thing I knew she never wanted. It looked huge, this blue plastic pipe that snaked out of a machine and into her perpetually forced-open mouth. She couldn't speak because of it, but she looked at me with her open eye and blinked in greeting. The other eye, the droopy-lidded one, was now, inexplicably, all the way shut. Her blue-and-white hospital nightgown had slipped off one shoulder, exposing part of her breast, as if she had been running away and her pursuer had been pulling at her clothes. I pulled it up and tucked it back around her shoulder.

Dr. M. talked with me and my three siblings—all of us having flown in from far away—in the corridor of the ICU. Red-haired, forty-something, he spoke in an uninflected voice as if to bring calm to a situation that wasn't calm at all. It was he who had taken out our mother's ruptured spleen when she arrived in the ambulance. He said that when she came into the emergency room, she had been not only conscious but irritable, and we took this to be a good sign. He explained that she had broken some ribs, fractured her collarbone and a bone in her neck, and badly bruised one lung. He said that if she were young and healthy she'd be able to recover from everything easily, but because of her age and the fact that her lungs were already compromised by emphysema, she had a struggle ahead.

Her friend, the driver, had been shaken but not seriously injured, and was released from the hospital wearing a neck brace.

"We're aiming to wean her off the ventilator as soon as we can," said Dr. M., "but her bruised lung will have to do some healing first."

It was clear to us she wanted to be unhooked. Her wrists were tethered to the bed rails to keep her from pulling out the breathing tube, but she kept raising an agitated hand in the direction of her mouth. A plastic clamp was wrapped around her face to hold the tube in place; it was tight across her upper lip, below her nose, and the pink flesh of her lip swelled out beneath it like a bubble. Whether she was awake or asleep, she always had one eye open and one eye closed, as if in simultaneous commitment to the dream world and the world of the ICU. She was heavily sedated, but when the nurse told her to wiggle her toes, she wiggled her toes.

We stood around the bed and sang, afraid to stop. We didn't know what to do if we weren't singing. We sang the songs our father used to sing, when we were children. All the songs seemed to be about death, but my mother wasn't paying attention to the words. Her heart rate slowed as we sang: "You are lost and gone forever, dreadful sorry, Clementine."

"Would you like me to rub your feet?" I asked when the song was over.

She nodded and I took one foot in both hands and stroked the smooth skin on the top, feeling my way along the bones to her toes. I could tell by the way she gave me the weight of her foot that it she liked it. I knew the look of her feet, of course, with their perfectly graduated toes, but I had never formed the thought: *My mother has beautiful feet.* Nor had I ever rubbed her feet before. My mother had had to put herself in the ICU to get me to come as close to her as she had always wanted.

My mother had written a living will, stating that she didn't wish life support to be continued if she was stuck in a comatose state, and she had sent us copies years before. A few days after the accident, we found another paper in her apartment—an undated note in our mother's handwriting saying, "Do NOT put a tube down my throat to keep me alive." The pressure of the pen had a commanding tone; I could hear my mother's voice. Upset, we showed the note to Dr. M.

"This is different," he said. "She was in a car accident—it's not as if we're keeping her alive in a vegetative state. I understand your concern, but she's getting better!"

"How long can a person be on a ventilator?" we asked.

"You don't want to go much more than two weeks," he said. "At that point we would recommend a tracheotomy if the patient still needs breathing support. But I don't foresee that happening in your mother's case. I hope to wean her off the ventilator in a few days."

OK, we could wait "a few days."

We slept, or tried to sleep, in our mother's apartment at the other end of the city, and we spent long days at the hospital. We took turns staying with her, watching the monitors, calling the nurses to raise or lower the bed, or to brush her mouth with a wet swab, surrendering ourselves to her care with an unfamiliar abandon. This room that was cluttered with medical equipment was miraculously swept clean of all our habitual impediments to love; I wasn't worried, for example, about what she thought of my hair.

"That clamp looks so tight on her upper lip," I said to the nurse.

"It has to be tight," the nurse said, "to keep her from pulling it out."

My mother was trying to communicate something: she was waving her arms, she leaned forward and shook her head in frustration, then fell back on the pillow, exhausted. A nurse brought a felt-tipped pen and a whiteboard, and we wrapped her fingers around the pen, but the marks she made were too wobbly to read, and the pen soon fell from her hand. Next we gave her a board with the alphabet on it, and her hand moved across the smooth surface like the pointer on a Ouija board, but it was hard to tell when she was stopping over a letter and when she was just on her way to another letter. We kept guessing the wrong letters, until she pushed away the letter board with a frustrated shrug.

We supposed she was trying to say something about the breathing tube. "We know you hate this tube, Mom, but we promise it's going to come out, and then you'll be able to say whatever you want!"

A few more days went by—it had been a week now—and we were told she had pneumonia, probably because of the breathing tube, and she was put on massive doses of antibiotics. This was a big bump in the road. They wouldn't be able to take the tube out until she got better from the pneumonia.

THE SECOND WEEK

A respiratory therapist came a couple of times a day to suction her out—a dreaded procedure. He pushed a tube the width of a straw down inside the wider ventilator tube, working it down, inch by inch, into my mother's lungs, as her left eye opened wider and wider in alarm, and even the heavy right lid lifted enough to show a slit of eyeball. I gave her my hand, and she squeezed it. Then came the bad part, when the RT pulled the little tube back out, creating suction. There was a rasping noise for a few seconds, like the sound a straw makes at the bottom of a milkshake, and my mother shuddered, and we watched the yellow phlegm come up through the translucent plastic tubing.

"Thank you, Alice," said the RT cheerfully.

My mother reached her sausage fingers up, trailing a wire that was clamped to her forefinger, and her hand came within inches of the breathing tube before it was stopped by the wrist restraint.

My brother and I took the elevator down to the hospital café for a break. There was no getting out of this situation—wherever I went I was always in it. Still, it was a relief to sit in the café downstairs, surrounded by the hum of strangers' voices and the clacking of food trays. "I feel like I've lived in this hospital all my life," I said.

"Yes, it seems like time has stopped," my brother said. The skin of his tired face looked like soft flannel.

"Well, she's going to get better or she's going to get worse," I said. This was an oddly comforting thought.

One morning when we came into the room, the breathing tube was attached with tape to our mother's chin, and there was a bandage on her upper lip. The nurse said, "I have bad news—the clamp made a hole in her lip. I'm terribly sorry. I've called down to plastic surgery—someone will be up later to look at her—I don't think it will seriously disfigure her." She lifted the bandage to show us a hole in our mother's lip the size of a dime—a window with a bloody frame, through which I could see gums and teeth. "Remember," the nurse said, "she's been heavily sedated, so I doubt it feels as bad as it looks."

———

On the ninth morning, a Tuesday, she looked paler and more remote than ever. Discouraged, we told Dr. M. we didn't know how much longer we could put her through this. "We're thinking about asking you to take that tube out now, whether she's ready or not."

He took us seriously. "I understand that you want to honor Alice's wishes, and I respect that. I won't stand in the way of whatever you decide. But she still has a good chance." He straightened up and spoke with a burst of fresh energy. "Give me until Friday! I'm making it my goal to get her off the ventilator by Friday."

Encouraged by the vigor of his new vow, we agreed to hang in there for three more days.

In the meantime, with Dr. M.'s support, we had an exploratory meeting with Dr. Z. from palliative care, in case the time came that we decided to withdraw life support. He was tall and thin, an angel of death in a white coat, and he described some possible scenarios in answer to our questions, but it was hard to absorb the information—it was so hypothetical. "Feel free to call on me again," he said as we shook hands all around. "I'm here to help you with your decisions, not to persuade you one way or the other."

As our mother's spirits went up and down, so did ours. We were adults in our fifties and sixties, parents ourselves, and yet our moods depended on whether our mother blinked at us when we spoke to her. I brought my laptop into the room and tried to attend to some business, but I couldn't concentrate on anything in the unreal world beyond the hospital. So I worked on crocheting a shawl for my mother—zigzag blue and green stripes, colors she liked.

Friday came and she still had a tube down her throat. She stared unblinking when I came into the room, and she didn't even wiggle her toes when the nurse asked her to. She still had pneumonia, and the numbers on the monitor had not improved. We didn't see Dr. M. all morning. This was clearly not the day she'd be liberated from the ventilator.

The four of us met in a windowless cubicle down the corridor called the Family Conference Room. "This is exactly what she never wanted," my sister said.

"He keeps saying just a few more days," my other sister said, "and then a few more days go by and she's worse, and then he says give me just a few more days."

My brother said, "She's *tied* to the bed—you know what I mean?" His voice broke. "We're her children, and we're *choosing* to put her through this."

Huddled together in that stuffy chamber, exhausted beyond all reason, we agreed it was time to let her go. We left word at the nurses' station that we wanted to talk to Dr. M.

We telephoned our children—her grandchildren. "We have to let her go," we sang, like sailors preparing to loose the mooring line from its bow cleat and drop it into the salty water.

My older son, the first grandchild, far away in Texas, said, "I thought she was getting *better*. Yesterday you said she was getting better." I was curled up on the floor under the pay phone in the waiting room.

"We thought she was," I said, "but today she's worse. If you could see her, all full of tubes, with her hands tied, just staring out with one eye open . . . She asked us not to put a tube down her throat. She's counting on us."

"But maybe the antibiotics just need more time to cure the pneumonia," he said.

"We're going to ask the doctor about that," I promised him.

Dr. M. came around at last, and we went out into the corridor to talk. When we told him we thought it was time to let her go, he seemed surprised. "Why today?" he asked.

"Well, it's *Friday*," I said. "You said you'd get her off the breathing tube by Friday."

"She's holding steady," he said. "I'd like to get her oxygen support down to forty percent, but the pneumonia is slowing us down."

"Shouldn't the antibiotics have gotten rid of the pneumonia by now?" my brother asked.

"I want to give them a few more days to work. I know you're worrying about keeping her on the ventilator, and I respect that. As I told you, I don't like to go more than two weeks with the ventilator, but it won't be two weeks until Monday."

We agreed to a third extension.

When we went back into the room, our mother was sitting up in bed, and for the first time since the accident she stretched her mouth into her version of a smile around the blue pipe. We looked at each other in amazement. Did she guess what we'd been saying in the hall?

We called the grandchildren back. We couldn't believe that a couple of hours before, we had decided this was to be her last day on earth.

THE THIRD WEEK

We wanted to help her rally her strength by Monday. I asked my son Noah to come from Texas to cheer her on, and the very next morning, Saturday, he walked into her hospital room. She brightened and reached her tethered hands toward him. He was a tall man now, and he leaned way down until she got her hands onto his shoulders, and she pulled him down into her bower of tubes to give him the fumbling kiss of a bridled horse. He held a picture of his two-month-old daughter, her first great-grandchild, in front of her open eye, and she studied it hard.

On Monday, after morning rounds, Dr. M. called us into the corridor outside our mother's room. "It looks like a good day for an extubation!" he said.

Quite a crowd of family members and medical people

gathered in the room for the big event, including Dr. Z., the one who helped patients die; his presence worried me.

"Hello, Alice," said Dr. M. "You'll be happy to hear that we're going to take out the breathing tube now. Are you ready for that?" She nodded enthusiastically.

It turned out there was nothing to it. The respiratory therapist pulled the tube out as easily as if she was pulling up a weed with a long root, and Mom was breathing.

The RT put an oxygen mask on her face to give her a little extra help in the transition. It was fastened around the back of her head with elastic, like a Halloween mask. They finally took off the wrist restraints.

Dr. M. had said she probably wouldn't talk right away because her vocal cords would be sore, but she was already lifting the mask and moving her lips, finding her voice after the long mute weeks. She was the diva and we, her eager audience, strained to hear. The words came out, one at a time, hoarse and irritated: "I just want to wipe my chin!"

Dr. M. was proud of her, and he brought a couple of the residents into the room to show her off to. Everybody was jubilant.

"Do you know where you are, Alice?" asked Dr. M.

"I'm not quite sure," she said. "Am I in the kitchen?"

He told her she was in the hospital. "And can you tell me how many grandchildren you have?"

"Nine," she said proudly. "I have nine grandchildren."

Dr. M. looked at me. "She does," I said.

"And do you remember," Noah asked her, "that you have a great-granddaughter?"

"Yes," she said proudly. "I certainly do remember *that*!"

Noah, having seen her over the hump, was ready to say good-bye. "You're getting better, Grandma! I'm coming back to Chicago in the spring, and I'll bring your new great-granddaughter to meet you!"

"I can't wait," my mother said. "That will be wonderful."

The day after the tube came out, a Tuesday, she told the nurse she wanted to turn on her side, and the nurse helped her do that. "It's time to get ready for the baby," she explained.

"You're not having a baby, Mom," I said.

"I know *that!*" she said, annoyed at my obtuseness. "I have to get ready for my great-*grandbaby*. I have to make a place for her." She curled up and made a half-moon of a nest in the bed for her great-granddaughter to lie beside her. She patted the spot.

"You'll see her in a few months," I said.

Dr. M. told us not to worry that our mother was sometimes confused. He said it was normal for a person who's been in the ICU for a while to become disoriented. It would go away, he said.

The next morning she was in a grateful mood. I was sitting in the corner crocheting when she waved her hand at the ceiling over her bed. "I'm giving you that one for a present," she told my sister.

"You mean that tile right there?" my sister asked, pointing to one of the six-inch square acoustic tiles over Mom's head. I was impressed that she had understood.

"Yes," Mom said, and turning to me, she continued, "that one's for you, and that one . . ." She gave each of her children the gift of a ceiling tile. She didn't have anything else to give.

On Wednesday, the third day off the ventilator, she seemed to be weakening. "What's going on?" we asked Dr. M.

"I don't know," he said. "We're delivering as much oxygen as we can through the mask, and she's just maintaining." He paused, as if gathering himself, and said, "You should think about what you want to do if she gets to the point where she won't make it without mechanical support. Would you want us to do a tracheotomy?"

Once the tube was out, we couldn't bear the thought of putting it back in, and we already had her instructions. Still, people can change their minds, and now that she could talk to us, we decided to ask her.

We waited for one of her brief windows of alertness. Dr. Z., the palliative care doctor, came into the room to support us. He pulled up a chair beside her bed, so he was at eye level with her. The rest of us stood around the bed, and my sister asked her that terrible question again and again: "Do you want us to put the tube back in if it turns out you'll die without it?" She asked in different ways, and our mother said nothing. We thought she didn't understand. Then Dr. Z. leaned in to help. "Alice, would you object if we put the breathing tube back in?"

"Yes, I would," she said quietly.

"Now listen carefully. If you need it to live and we don't put the tube back in, you'll die. If that happens, we'll make you comfortable. How do you feel about that?"

She suddenly sat up in the bed and exclaimed, "Shit! This is a lousy time to ask a question like that!" Then, as if to explain her loss of temper, she added in a softer voice, "I've already discussed these matters with my children."

On Thursday morning she perked up a little—she could still be getting better. One of my nieces, visiting from college, brought her violin into the room. "Want me to play something for you, Grandma?" she asked.

"Yes, play me something cheerful," said my mother.

So my niece played a Scottish tune called "Ships Are Sailing," and my mother tapped her fingers on the bedrail in time, to show her pleasure.

But that afternoon she became increasingly anxious and agitated, shaking her shoulders, waving her hands, shifting her legs. Her breathing got faster and shallower. "Just breathe slow and easy, Mom, just slow and easy," I said, and though my words couldn't put more oxygen into her lungs, they calmed us both for a moment.

Dr. M. relinquished her as his patient to Dr. Z. who put her on a morphine drip to relieve her feeling of air hunger. Dr. Z. said she'd be more comfortable on the palliative care floor, and my sisters and brother were ready for the transition. "But isn't that giving up on her?" I asked.

Dr. Z. said that they could do everything in palliative care to help her live that they could do for her down below, and she would be more comfortable besides. So I agreed, telling myself it wasn't beyond the realm of possibility that she could still get better.

The next day, Friday, a bed became available in palliative care—meaning I suppose, that someone had died—and in the afternoon my mother was moved to a hotel-like room on the sixteenth floor, the top floor of the hospital, closest to heaven, with fabric drapes and upholstered armchairs. She had always held a good view to be one of life's greatest pleasures, and so, even though the morphine had put her to sleep and she seemed to see nothing out of her still-open eye, we wheeled her bed around so that she faced the picture window looking east, over the stone turrets and steel roofs of Chicago to the darkening expanse of Lake Michigan.

Dr. Z. said it could take several hours or several days for her to die. It was a relief to get her out of the technological brambles of the ICU, though the monitor that measured her blood gases was still hooked up, and I was still watching it, as if there was meaning in it.

Out in the hall I told Dr. Z., "Her oxygen level keeps going down to eighty."

He put his hand on my arm. "Mom is dying," he told me in the voice of a kindergarten teacher. "Now is the time to make her comfortable." I knew he was trying to be kind, but I spun away from him and marched down the hall—she wasn't *his* "Mom."

But it wasn't really his use of the word *Mom* that was upsetting me; it was the rest of the sentence.

There were six of us family members in the room—children and grandchildren—when the palliative care nurse took off the oxygen mask and put on the nasal cannula: "She'll be more comfortable." I looked back and forth from my mother's face to the monitor, and I saw the numbers drop like an elevator—into the seventies, sixties, fifties. My son Sandy was sitting across the room in an armchair. "Grandma's dying," I heard myself say, and he jumped up to join us at the bedside. Helpless, we watched her sternum rise and fall like the prow of a ship in heavy seas; helpless, we watched her face turn white as the red blood drained out of the capillaries.

In less than two minutes she stopped breathing. We stood there, waiting for something to happen, waiting for our mother to tell us what to do next. But she had left the room. I don't know how she managed this disappearing act—I never saw her get up and go, and I was beside her the whole time. After a pause, all six of us began to cry. It was ten o'clock on a Friday night.

The nurse slipped out while we wept, and after a polite absence of ten minutes or so, she came back in with some papers for us to sign. "You can stay here with the body for two hours," she said. "Then we have to remove it." Time swung around and slammed into a wall. How suddenly the nurse's patient had turned into a body. Now that my mother was truly comfortable, the nurse's job was done.

We took off her neck brace—there was a red sore underneath where it had been rubbing against her collarbone. We sang "Dona Nobis Pacem" and "Row Row Row Your Boat." I recited a Buddhist chant for the dying, and the ancient sounds we didn't understand held us together: *nen nen fu ri shin*. My sisters and I took her clothes out of a plastic bag, the clothes she'd been wearing in the accident. It seemed strange, though it was a relief, that there was no blood on them. Together we took off the hospital nightgown and pulled her faded black denim pants up over her dead hips, we put her arms through the sleeves of her blue smock shirt, and we left her bare feet bare. Her face looked suddenly thin, the skin drawn by gravity down toward the pillow. We tried to close her open mouth, but it didn't stay. The same with her open eye. We folded her hands on her chest, and I spread the half-finished shawl with the zigzag blue and green stripes over her legs.

# Old Bones

I TOOK MY ALMOST-THREE granddaughter to the play-ground, and she climbed *up* the slide on her hands and knees.

"Now *you* do it, Grandma Sue," she said.

"I can't do it," I told her. "My old knees can't go up the slide."

"Just try! You can just *try*, Grandma!"

But I didn't try. "I'm sorry, Paloma, but my knees are too old."

The next day I was taking Paloma upstairs to have a bath. "Carry me, OK, Grandma?" she requested.

I was tired. "You can walk," I said. "I'll hold your hand."

"I can't do it," she said. "I have old legs!"

As I get older my bones are getting older, too. I have osteoporosis in my lower back. It runs in my family. My mother lost five inches of height from it, and I've lost an inch and a half, but it doesn't hurt and I wouldn't even know I had it except for the bone scan.

The arthritis in my knees and thumbs is more annoying. At the minor-detail end of the scale, I can't open jars very well any more because of the arthritis in my thumbs, and this can be bothersome when I'm alone with a vacuum-sealed jar of homemade plum jam. A friend gave me a wonderful gizmo, like a potholder, with rubber webbing on one side, which is remarkably effective for opening jars, but if it doesn't do the job and there's no other pair of hands in the house, I have to get through the morning without jam. As for my knees, they don't like going up and down steep hills, they object to the warrior pose in yoga, and I can't squat at all anymore, which makes it hard to pee in the woods. Hopscotch is out of the question.

In a way, it adds interest to life to have these small problems to work on. Taking care of oneself becomes a more intricate project and sharpens one's problem-solving skills. My knees talk to me, and I have to respond. The old bones provide a kind of companionship. It's not really me who needs things like handrails and hiking poles, it's my knees; I make these arrangements for them, because we're family.

Without spending my whole life reading about it on the Internet, I try to learn how to take care of my bones. For years I took a drug prescribed for promoting bone density. Over a year ago I decided to stop, because of the slight risk of serious side effects, and I promised myself I would care for my bones as best I could by taking calcium and vitamin D and doing daily, or almost daily, weight-bearing exercise—in my case walking and working out at the Y. After a year on my new program, I asked for another bone scan. I was proud of myself when the test showed that the osteoporosis had not gotten any worse. I'm my own research project.

I used to take my bones for granted, but now that I'm paying attention to them, I see that they are a great invention. When young people's bones are growing, for example, cells get added to the outside of the lengthening bone at the same time that cells are subtracted from the inside, in order to enlarge the hollow part where the marrow lives, in a complex engineering project. When I was about twelve, my leg bones were growing so fast that I got terrible leg aches. My mother called them "growing pains."

Both of my sons also had leg pains during their adolescent growth spurts.

Now I'm shrinking. Under the soft flesh, the bones are shorter, lighter, more porous than they used to be, with spurs here and there that were not part of the original design. But they are still good bones—hinges and sockets, ball bearings and cables. I love their names: humerus, tibia, scapula, fibula.

One time when my son Sandy was a teenager, he and I were hiking along some abandoned railroad tracks in the country and we noticed lots of dry bones—the scattered vertebrae of some large animal, probably a deer—lying on the ties between the rails. We collected them all in our pockets and took them back to the cabin where we were staying for the weekend. We spread them out on the table like the pieces of a puzzle. The hollow round bones had little feet and outspread wings and they fit together neatly, like stacking chairs. We were impressed by the elegance of the design and we could distinguish different sections of the spine by the size of the wings, and whether they had dorsal fins. A few were missing. We found string and scissors and made the bones into a mobile, balancing pendant chains of vertebrae against a rusty railroad spike. We hung it up in our friend's cabin, happy with the way the old bones swung in the sun.

None of the vertebrae are missing on the human skeleton that hangs from a hook in the yoga studio I go to. It looks so perfect, like it was made from a kit as a visual aid for a yoga class, that it's easy to forget it used to walk around inside a particular person. I wonder who.

When you check "donor" on your driver's license, it doesn't mean you're donating your bones to a yoga studio. You would really be naked in public, then. Still, nobody would know it was you, unless there was a little brass plaque on the pelvis with your name. Nobody would recognize your skeleton, not even your best friend, not even someone who had made love to you for years.

It's odd that skeletons and skulls represent death, since,

if you're a living human being, you have your very own living skeleton inside you, and it holds you up your whole life long. You'd be a puddle on the floor without it. I guess a skeleton means death because you can't *see* a skeleton until the person is dead and the flesh has fallen away.

At the celebration of the Day of the Dead in Oaxaca, I saw skeletons dancing, skeletons working at their sewing machines and typewriters, skeletons cutting the hair of other skeletons in the barber shop. I brought home a little scene of a doctor skeleton delivering a baby skeleton from a mother skeleton while a nurse skeleton stands ready to assist.

You know you're going to die, and you don't know what's going to happen to you after that. You also don't know what's going to happen to you before that, as a result of age, and you can't control it. A young friend of mine in medical school was told that the age of sixty is a kind of watershed, and that the average human body crosses a line about that time and begins to deteriorate in earnest. Of course doctors don't tell their patients this, and of course the age varies from one individual to another, but on the *average*, there is significant change at sixty.

For a sixtieth birthday present, my two sons promised to take me backpacking in the Sierra. I had taken them camping and backpacking often when they were children, and this time they would be my outfitters and guides. The promise alone was one of the best presents I ever received, and then there would be the trip itself on top of the promise. For a couple of months before the trip I worked out extra hard at the gym. I had several sessions with a personal trainer, who mercilessly made me climb stairs that fell away beneath my feet and step up and down on purple plastic boxes to strengthen my quads for hiking.

My sons plotted the route, got the permits, rented the tent, planned the menus, and bought the food. On the appointed day, Sandy and I drove together from the Bay Area and Noah drove from Los Angeles to our meeting point in the town of Bishop, on the east side of the Sierra. I was excited when we pulled into the parking lot of the ranger station and saw Noah's blue Toyota, shimmering in the August heat. We found Noah inside the ranger station, where he'd arrived just fifteen minutes before, looking at flower books. We got our fire permit and rented the required bear-proof cylinder for our food, and at the last minute, before we set off for the trailhead, I followed Sandy's suggestion and bought myself a pair of hiking poles. I also bought, on a sudden impulse, a tiny booklet on the U.S. Constitution that was placed prominently next to the cash register. This was during George W. Bush's presidency, when the Constitution was under siege, and I thought it might come in handy somewhere down the line, if not in the High Sierra.

My legs felt strong as we set forth. We hiked up high and moved camp each day. I took small steps and made my own little switchbacks when the trail was steep, and sometimes my muscles felt wobbly after a long climb, but I managed just fine. My two strapping sons carried the heavier packs and kindly kept to a gentle pace, claiming it was what they wanted, too. We swam in little lakes along the way, and admired the flowers, and watched the clouds scud over the mountains. We hardly saw any other hikers; most of the time the three of us had the trail to ourselves. And not just the trail. We had the universe, as far as we could see, and that was far indeed, and there was no one else I would rather have been with.

My renovated quadriceps took me and my backpack up and over Paiute Pass, twelve thousand feet above sea level. On the third day we found our own miniature alpine meadow, sheltered from the wind by granite boulders, beside Lower Desolation Lake. After the tent was up, Noah and Sandy went to explore Upper Desolation Lake and I lay on my back in the grass, surrounded by yellow arnica flowers, letting the afternoon sun soak into my sore knees. The strange trill of a marmot bounced off the rocky slope above me. My bones had been working against gravity all day, and now they laid themselves out on the mountain; the long vertical bones became horizontal, and gravity took them and held them. I took a nap.

The next day we headed back over Paiute Pass. We paused to look back at the lake, steel gray under a threatening sky, and I managed to balance my camera on a rock and take a picture of the three of us, grinning and holding onto each other, dizzy in all that space. Before we started down, I looked hard at the wide bowl the mountains made, taking a picture of it with my mind, the kind of picture you can't take with a camera, one that has the smell of the wind in it and the relief your shoulders feel when you give them a break from the weight of the pack. I knew I might never see such a view again.

I was grateful for my hiking poles—my knees needed all the help they could get now that we were going down. Noah and Sandy took from my pack the little bit of common gear I was still carrying, along with my camera, sunscreen, and extra flashlight batteries. Each of their packs was probably twice as heavy as mine.

In the late afternoon, as we were descending a steep and rocky slope above tree line, it began to snow. There was no level place to camp, and so we had to keep going down, while the wet snow kept on coming and the sky grew darker. We hurried slowly—my steps got smaller as my knees got sorer, and the trail was slippery. I was slowing them down, but they didn't make me feel bad about it; they were patient, asking from time to time how I was doing. Other than that we hardly spoke, focusing our attention numbly on the trail. We were eager to get the tent up before dark.

Just at dusk, we came to a rocky field, and with frozen fingers we pitched the tent on a level spot of ground that didn't have too many bumps to poke into our backs. By the time the tent was up we were wet and cold and hungry, and it was almost dark and still snowing. We took our packs inside the tent and put on some dry clothes, but then we felt the sloshing of water beneath us. It turned out there was no drainage where we'd pitched the tent, and it was already sitting in its own private lake of melted snow. We all crawled out again, and while Noah dug a drainage ditch around the tent with the plastic trowel we'd brought for our bathroom needs, Sandy went into the mostly imaginary shelter of a nearby grove of bristlecone pines to heat water on our stove for our freeze-dried dinner of macaroni and cheese. I held the flashlight.

I wondered: What if the storm blew our tent down in the middle of the night and we died of hypothermia? Or what if it snowed so much that we couldn't hike out for days? Or what if we just couldn't find the trail under the snow and got lost? But I didn't speak my thoughts aloud.

"Dinner is ready," said Sandy. "I have a reservation for a party of three."

I can't say we enjoyed our dinner, but we stood together there in the trees and eagerly spooned the hot soup out of our Sierra cups—the very Sierra cups that still had our Yahi Indian names engraved on them from a school camping trip with Noah's fifth-grade class twenty-five years before. I had gone as a parent helper—with knees that could scramble over boulders with the kids—and Sandy had gone as a little brother. As it said on the cups, we were Tetna, Siwini, Wakara: Bear, Pine, and Full Moon.

Then there was nothing to do but crawl into the tent, and into our sleeping bags, and try to stay warm. It was eight o'clock at night in the middle of August, and morning was a long way away. We wished we had brought a pack of cards, but we hadn't anticipated our predicament. All we had for indoor entertainment was the U.S. Constitution, so while more snow fell and drifted up against the sides of our tent, we quizzed each other on the Bill of Rights.

By the time we got back down to the car the next day, my right knee was protesting with every step, and both feet were aching with what turned out to be heel spurs. I was also completely happy.

Five years have gone by since then, and it seems that it was, indeed, the last such adventure of my life. Cortisone shots took care of the heel spurs, but the arthritis in my knees has gradually gotten worse. That's what arthritis tends to do. And why wouldn't it? It's hard work for those joints to carry a body up and down mountains, up and down stairs, year after year. At least I ended my backpacking days on a high note, and I'm still capable of ascending into the mountains by mule or funicular.

It's a constant process, letting go of what you can no longer do, and stretching yourself to do what you can. When I was sixty-three, I went to a series of hip-hop dance classes at the YMCA, for beginners. There were a couple of other graying students in the class, though I think I was the grayest. It was challenging for me, both physically and cognitively, and I could almost feel new neural pathways being laid down in my brain as we went from the stomp to the spin-and-turn.

One day the teacher had us scooting across the room in a grapevine step. I thought I was safe in the back row, but when he told us turn around and go the other way, I was suddenly in the front row. I scurried like mad but I couldn't keep up—I was in the way, holding up the line. The teacher escorted me to a different spot in the room and had me trade places with a supple young man.

"I think you'll be better off here," the teacher told me. Then, in front of the whole class, he said, "You looked like this!" and he imitated me stumbling across the room.

I could have said, "Hey! You're talking to the person who won the javelin throw in the fourth grade!" But oddly, I didn't really mind his teasing. For a moment I seemed to float up out of my stiff body and drift beside the high windows of the room. I looked down with affection at my sixty-three-year-old self, struggling to learn hip-hop dancing, and I could see that there was something humorous in my efforts to get my feet to crisscross fast enough. I gave myself credit for trying, but I didn't go back to hip hop after that. Time to let that one go.

———

I'm still using my own old knees and feeling loyal to them, but I might get a couple of new knees down the line, and I'm grateful the possibility exists. In the meantime, it looks like I'll be able to keep on with my yoga class for a good while to come, and I and my hiking poles still walk with pleasure in the Berkeley hills.

Paloma recently imitated me, too, though she wasn't teasing like the hip-hop teacher; she was, by her tone of voice, just making a friendly observation. We were taking a walk around the block to look for ladybugs, and she said, "Look Grandma, I'm walking like you." She adopted a stiff-legged gait, not bending her knees at all, like those Appalachian wooden dolls who walk down an incline board. I was taken aback. Was my stiff old walk really that obvious? But as far as Paloma was concerned there was nothing wrong with it; it was just my way of walking.

# All Fall Down

A fall is an unintentional loss of balance causing one to make unexpected contact with the ground or floor.

—*Journal of the American Geriatrics Society*, Vol. 39

THE LAST TIME I FELL DOWN, I was at a Zen meditation retreat. About twenty meditators had gathered in a silent circle on a raised deck in the redwoods for our daily work meeting, and I remember thinking as I walked down the path to join the gathering that my shoes were too big. A few steps short of the deck, in full view of the silent watchers, I slipped on the uneven path. I felt my ankle twisting as I went down. It's amazing how much you can think about in the split second between tripping and hitting the ground. On my way down I was already worrying that someone would have to leave the retreat and drive me to Sebastopol to get my ankle x-rayed, but that thought was interrupted when my face slammed into the edge of the deck. A collective wail went up from my audience. It didn't hurt, not exactly—it was too much of a shock. My attention moved from my ankle to my face in a groping attempt to understand what had happened. It was something to do with my mouth. Teeth—Did I still have my teeth? My hand came away from my lips bloody, but my teeth all seemed to be still attached to my guns.

I uncurled from the ground and looked up into a crowd of faces leaning over the deck railing. "I'm all right," I said. "I'm really all right." *How could this be me in a heap on the ground? I'm a tree-climber, a jump-roper, a gravity-defier.* "I feel like such an idiot!" I added. (It's this inability to admit that one is getting old that makes it so hard to get around to installing handrails and buying non-skid rubber bath mats.)

Hands reached out and pulled me up. One fellow meditator, a nurse, led me to wash up. She couldn't find any ice, but she found a cucumber in the fridge and sliced it in half for me to hold against my bloody lip. Soothed by her ministrations, I returned to the group for my work assignment, and that afternoon I performed my duty as a tea server in the meditation hall. A swollen lip doesn't stop a person from pouring tea.

The physical damage was insignificant—some colorful bruises that faded away in a week. I got a lot of kind attention and many offers of arnica. But it was scary to hit the deck like that, face first.

I've taken some other falls since turning sixty, and so I decided to do some Internet research about falling. I found lots of useful bits of advice, like, "Don't stand on chairs, tables, or boxes," from the Public Health Agency of Canada's Division of Aging and Seniors. Another good suggestion: "Try to land on your buttocks to prevent more serious injuries." From the Centers for Disease Control came the advice I should have heeded to prevent that last fall: "Wear shoes that give good support and have non-slip soles."

I learned that about thirteen thousand people age sixty-five and over die every year in the United States as the result of a fall—that's thirty-five a day. Many more are injured and their health is compromised.

Preventing falls in seniors turns out to be an entire field

of medicine unto itself. And I was astonished to learn that for several years in a row, a bill was introduced to Congress called the Keeping Seniors Safe from Falls Act, though it was never passed. Who would vote against such a bill? It must have been too expensive.

In addition to just plain falling, the *fear* of falling is bad for the health, keeping people in their chairs, where their muscles get weaker and weaker. Again, from the Canadian Division of Aging, "Do not let the fear of falling prevent you from being active. Inactivity creates an even greater risk of falling."

The first of what I think of as my age-related falls happened because I was engaging in behavior that was not age-appropriate. It was a gorgeous summer day, and I was riding on a narrow bike path behind my ten-year-old niece, who was out of sight. I'm not too old to ride a bike, but I felt suddenly compelled to ride "no hands" as I used to do when I was a girl of ten. *You're only as old as you feel!* Aren't they always telling you that? The carefree breeze caressed my hair and the warblers seemed to be singing my praises from the bushes, until my wheel slipped on some gravel at a curve in the path and down I went, skinning my knees, hands, and elbows. Wheeling my bike, I limped to where my niece waited for me at a fork in the path. "My God! What happened to you?" she exclaimed.

"Pride goeth before a fall," I told her. I have given up riding "no hands" for the rest of my life—one more age-related loss. At least this one is easy to live with.

The truth is, my balance is bad. In my yoga class, I stand near the wall for the crane pose and surreptitiously touch it with a knee or an elbow, as no self-respecting crane would ever do. My yoga teacher has told me you can improve your balance with practice. So I've adopted a daily practice. Every morning, while I use my electric toothbrush, which turns itself off after exactly two minutes, I stand on one foot. On the even dates I stand on the right foot and on the odd dates I stand on the left. The calf muscles of the standing foot burn. At first I couldn't make it through two minutes, but now I can.

As I get older the ground seems to get farther and farther away, and it takes longer for my brain to get the signals to my feet, and vice versa. Sometimes when I first get out of bed in the morning I stumble against the door frame on my way to the bathroom. My body used to take care of ordinary things like walking on its own, without adult supervision; now I have to think about picking up my feet.

I realize that a cane is not just to support weak joints and muscles—it helps you balance. I'm not there yet, though I do use hiking poles, and there's no loss of pride in that because even young and athletic people use them. I have a cane of my grandfather's in the attic, waiting for me. It's made of some kind of bone. And after canes come walkers.

Speaking of walkers, I've been watching a friend's ten-month-old learn to walk. She holds onto the coffee table and walks herself along its edge, and then she takes the great plunge, lets go, and steps out across space, two full steps to the edge of the sofa! Triumph! As for me, I'm moving in the opposite direction. Someday the people in the room may clap for me, too, as I let go of the edge of the kitchen table and take the bold step across space to the kitchen counter.

My friend's daughter falls down frequently in the process of learning to walk, and she bounces back up on her rubber skeleton. Sometimes she cries, but it never lasts long. When you are over sixty and the ground spins up into your face, it's a different story, especially when your bones are getting porous, as mine are.

While staying in a friend's rustic cabin, I got up in the middle of the night to use the outhouse. Returning to bed in the moonless, nightlight-less dark, I tripped and fell against a wooden platform and, as I later learned, broke two ribs. The crash awoke the young woman sleeping at the other end of the loft, who kindly asked what she could do to help, but I could think of nothing, and I since I had had the good fortune to fall *after* visiting the outhouse, I went back to bed, took an aspirin, and slept until morning.

If you're going to break bones, ribs are the best bones to break. For a few weeks, it hurt to cough or laugh, but it's amazing how well the body works. I just went on with my life, trying not to cough, and after a while my ribs weren't broken anymore. How do they know how to fix themselves? When my car gets a dent, it keeps a dent.

After my mother's death, my siblings and I packed up her belongings in her apartment in Chicago. When we were done, I said good-bye to my sister, who waited for the movers among boxes in the empty, echoing living room, and I left the apartment for the last time, to head back home to California. It was a bitter winter day as I trundled my way along the sidewalk with suitcase and tote bag. When I was half a block from the bus stop, I saw a bus approaching and I began to run. I slipped and fell on the icy sidewalk and papers and books went flying out of my tote bag. My hands were badly scraped and bloody, and one knee was skinned under my torn pants. As I struggled to my feet, I saw the bus pull away.

Two women coming along the sidewalk caught up with me—angels of kindness. "Are you all right? Can we help you?" One brushed the leaves off my back, and the other picked up my papers.

"I'm OK," I said. The part of me that wasn't OK was invisible—it had to do with leaving my mother's apartment behind for the last time. It had to do with the fact that she was dead. She'd taken her final fall; we had returned her ashes to the ground.

I thanked the women and walked to the bus stop, just as another bus pulled up. I got on, fumbled for my money with my bloody hands, and sat down in disarray. I must have looked pretty bad to the people on the bus, but once I was settled for the long ride to the airport, I wiped the blood off my hands with a handkerchief I'd taken from my mother's top dresser drawer.

A happier fall took place on my own front steps. Near the bottom, I unaccountably stepped off into the air when there was still one more step to go, and I fell hard on the concrete sidewalk. I rolled onto my back, feeling a fire burning in my ankle. It was a quiet morning in the neighborhood. No one was around. Nothing seemed to be broken. I lay there, stopped in my tracks on the way to the grocery store, looking up at the clear sky and the diagonal of the roofline jutting into it. I admired the top of the chimney. Time stopped, and I rested like a kindergartener at naptime. I had fallen not just down the steps but through a hole in the earth to a country without grocery stores, beyond the reach of gravity. I couldn't fall any farther. When the burning in my ankle subsided and I got up, relinquishing the moment of peace, I found that I could walk fine.

But there are other ways to find a peaceful moment. One of the items on all the lists of how to prevent falls is: "Have handrails installed on all staircases," and after that fall I finally got around to installing a handrail on the front steps. I'd been putting it off—could there really be someone living at my address who needs a handrail?—but now the smooth round wood feels good in my hand. It's almost as satisfying as sliding down the banister.

# Senior Moment, Wonderful Moment

I CALLED MY FRIEND Cornelia, a fellow grandmother, to ask if I could borrow a crib for my granddaughter's upcoming visit. When she answered the phone, I said, "Hi, Cornelia—it's Sue," and then my mind went blank. I paused, hopefully, but no more words came out of my mouth.

"Morning," she said. "What's up?"

She was a good enough friend that I didn't have to fake it, but still, it was unsettling. "Ummm," I said, waiting for the old neurons to start firing up again. I asked myself if it had to do with our weekly walking date. No-o-o . . . Was it about her son's article on stream conservation? No-o-o . . . Out the window a squirrel was running along the porch railing with a walnut in his mouth. "I'm having a senior moment," I said finally. "Do *you* happen to know why I called?"

She laughed. "You must have known that I have some plums to give you, from my tree." The squirrel was now sitting on the railing, peeling the outer shell off the walnut and spitting it on the ground. I'd never noticed before how the long fur of their tails waves back and forth like grass when they flick them.

By the time I went over to Cornelia's house to pick up the plums, I had remembered about the crib and I got that, too.

The Buddhist teacher Thich Nhat Hanh helps me appreciate my senior moments. In his book, *Present Moment, Wonderful Moment*, he writes, "The real miracle is to be awake in the present moment." I'm confident he would agree that a senior moment, a moment of forgetting what day it is or where you are going, can be a moment of deep understanding.

For example, standing in the kitchen wondering why I have a pair of scissors in my hand, I notice the sunlight glinting off its metal blades and dancing on the wall, and I repeat Nhat Hanh's sentence to myself: "The real miracle is to be awake in the present moment!" Younger people can also experience such transcendent moments of deep immersion in the infinite present, but they have to go to much greater lengths to do so, meditating for days at a time, for example, or hang gliding. I have only to carry a pair of scissors from one room to another.

I started out on a hike with friends, and when the path turned steeply and unexpectedly upward, I had to send them on without me, knowing my knees would not be able to bring me back down. I sat on a rock before returning to the lodge. This was not what we usually think of as a senior moment, but I speak of it here because it was another occasion when the frailty of age dropped me into a gap in time. I listened to my friends' voices, to their twig-snapping and leaf-rustling, until I could hear them no longer. I was cross at my knees for making me miss the companionship, though I knew they hadn't done it on purpose. I watched a yellow leaf twist its way down to the ground, and I heard it land on another leaf. Have you ever heard a leaf land on another leaf? OK—it wasn't the most exciting moment of my life, but it was good enough, and I wasn't missing it.

I say, "I'm having a senior moment" when I blow it, hoping to fend off the irritation of others with humor. But the next time the blankness comes over me, I'll try to be bold and move beyond self-deprecation. I'll say, "Senior moment, wonderful moment!" in order to remind the people around me of the wisdom that is to be found in these little coffee breaks of the brain.

A friend of mine takes another tack. He tells me he memorizes a stock phrase and keeps it handy to fill the gaps. So, if he's saying to an acquaintance over lunch, "Have you ever noticed that . . ." and he suddenly forgets the rest of the sentence, he brings out his all-purpose phrase: "It's incredibly hard to get the wrapper off a new CD." Or if he sees two old friends who don't know each other at a party, and their names vanish into the yawning void when the moment comes to introduce them, he shakes hands enthusiastically and says it again: "It's incredibly hard to get the wrapper off a new CD!" Like a pebble striking bamboo in an old Zen koan, his shocking statement offers his listeners a wake-up call to be here now.

It's not my fault when I have a senior moment any more than it was my fault when my hair turned gray. I'm just a human being, after all. I've had a lifetime of junior moments, when one word follows another in logical—and boring—succession, when each action leads to the next appropriate action. For countless years, I have remembered to bring the pencil with me when I go downstairs to use the pencil sharpener. I think I've earned the right to break free from the imprisonment of sequential thinking.

A senior moment is a stop sign on the road of life. It could even be a leg up toward enlightenment. So I stay calm, let the engine idle, and enjoy the scenery. What happens next will be revealed in due course.

PART TWO

*Changing Relationships*

# In the Shade of My Own Tree

WHEN I WAS A CHILD, we used to play "Old Maid," matching up pairs of cards until the loser was left with the only card that had no mate—the old maid card. The old maid's spectacles perched at the end of a long bony nose, twigs of hair stuck out from her bun, and she had a big mole on her chin. This image, which it didn't occur to me to question, struck a certain dread in my heart, and now, here I am, an old maid myself. Granted, in the strict sense of the word I'm not a *maid*, but I'm old and not married.

When I was a teenager, the models I had of older single women—we even used the word *spinster* back then—were not much more appealing to me than the old maid card. My high school education in a girls' prep school was delivered to me almost entirely by spinsters. I think of Miss Biddle, Miss Beveridge, Mlle. Casals, and our gym teachers, the Misses Sullivan and Bailey. They all tended to be shaped the same, like boards, with no hips and high shoulders, and I saw them as utterly sexless. They seemed to me to have washed up on the shores of that old-fashioned girls' school like flotsam. A callow teenage girl, I never wondered if they were lonely on Saturday nights.

Now I think of those teachers of mine with affection and sadness.

It's hard to be an older woman without a partner. I know from talking to friends that I'm not the only one who occasionally wakes up in the middle of the night alone in her bed and asks herself: *Wait a minute! How the hell did this happen?* Three in the morning is the loneliest time. What if the Big Earthquake comes right then and I've got no one to hold on to?

The world I live in puts people in pairs. We are taught to think in binary terms, to believe Plato's story that human beings were originally just one sex, and then were divided in two, and ever since, the two halves of one complete being are incomplete until they find each other.

This belief is affirmed by the earnest couples whose faces appear beside each other on book jackets. These experts on finding enlightenment through partnership smile into each other's eyes, and they declare right there on the back cover that the deepest understanding of what it means to be a human being can only be achieved through intimate partnership. Could it be that that's only one of the ways?

Even if you put enlightenment aside, there's still the need for simple animal companionship. When I broke a bone in my left shoulder not so many years ago, I could only sleep on my right side with my injured left arm carefully balanced on my torso like dead weight. When I lay down in bed at night, my good right arm was pinned under me, and it was a miserable moment when I realized that I couldn't do the simple and comforting thing that came next: I couldn't pull the covers up over myself. I felt keenly the absence of a person who had promised to stay with me in sickness and in health, who had vowed before witnesses to pull up the covers. I had to learn to hold the covers in my teeth while I lowered myself down on my good arm.

And those teachers of mine—I wonder now if anyone came to help them when they broke a bone. I wonder if any of them had loving friendships. Were they perhaps lesbians? Might any of them have chosen not to marry in order to devote their lives to mentoring young women?

One of them, the tiny Miss Punderson, with her sparkling blue eyes and thick white hair in a bun, made a surprising escape from spinsterhood. She had taught Chaucer and Milton to my mother a generation before and seemed to be an immortal spinster. But she retired at age sixty-five, the same year I graduated from the school, returned to her native Stockbridge, Massachusetts, and stunned us by marrying her old friend, the widowed painter Norman Rockwell. Could such a thing possibly happen to me? It's highly unlikely according to statistics; the older a single woman gets the harder it becomes to find a partner.

When my last long-term relationship ended, I was in my mid-fifties. I feared I had passed over a certain invisible threshold and that my marketability was way down. I worried about the critical density of wrinkles on the face, sagginess under the chin, brown spots on the back of the hands. It seemed that this complex arithmetic of signals was registered in a flash by single males of the species, whereupon they would turn away to talk to a younger woman if there was one about. The men my age were getting wattles, too, but I didn't look away from them.

As I anticipated turning sixty, I felt a new sense of urgency. If I really wanted to have a partner, I figured I'd better get busy, before the wrinkles around my mouth branched into my very lips. Afraid of being alone when I was really and truly old, I wanted to find someone who would have me before I moved on from the stage of gently faded gray to the even less marriageable stage of acrid breath. I wanted to find someone who, later on, could push my wheelchair, if it came to that. (I kept forgetting that if I did manage to hook up with a man my age, it might be just in time for me to start pushing *his* wheelchair.)

I embarked on a bout of dating, looking, as a friend put it, for "Codger Right." I called a dating service that advertised on the classical music station on the radio, so it had a veneer of propriety. They used to arrange dinners for three men and three women.

The woman who answered the phone asked my age, and when I told her I was fifty-nine she said, in a warm but business-like voice, "I'm sorry, but currently we're not taking any women over fifty-two." I asked her what age men they were "taking," but she wouldn't tell me.

A lesbian couple who are my friends met and fell in love at the age of sixty-five. They told me, "You have plenty of time!" They encouraged me to consider women, reminding me that women generally don't mind the wrinkles as much as men do. I said, "I had some experience with that years ago, and I found out I'm not really a lesbian." They said, "Sex doesn't have to be all that important. It's nice, but it's a small part of the show." Still, it didn't seem right to decide to be a lesbian solely because I had despaired of attracting a man.

I consulted the personal ads and set bravely forth on several blind dates. In one of my last efforts, I "went out for coffee" with an enthusiastic hiker and cyclist in his sixties, who did environmental consulting work. He seemed like a nice man. His wife of thirty-four years had died of cancer, and after two years of grieving, he was turning his attention to the world of dating. It made me like him that he had waited those two years.

He asked what had gone wrong with my marriage. That was a long time ago, I said. It was hard to stay married in Berkeley in the seventies. Nobody even believed in marriage.

He wanted to know what had gone wrong with my last relationship. Well, I said, I needed more independence in my life than he could make room for, and he needed more domestic companionship than I could give him.

So what had gone wrong with the relationships in between? I mumbled about being a single mother and the difficulties of balancing the needs of children and a boyfriend.

Then he wanted to know what made me think any relationship was ever going to work. Why was I answering ads? Why had I called him? "I'm just an ordinary person," he said. "I'm probably not any better than any of the others. Supposing we became involved, why should I imagine you'd want to stay with me?"

That brought me up short. "I hope I've learned from my mistakes," I said. "How did you stay with your wife all that time?"

"It was the commitment to the marriage," he said. "We never questioned our commitment, even in the rough times."

Before he wheeled his bike down the sidewalk, he said he didn't think there was much point in us meeting again.

It was hard, after a conversation like that, not to blame myself.

I called together a group of women friends my age who were single to talk about our situation. I wanted to know how they faced the challenge. We had a potluck lunch and sat in the sun and talked. We shared lonely feelings: "I don't know what my identity is without a partner," said one. Another said, "I miss the container of a relationship."

And we encouraged each other, too. One woman said she talked to a good friend every day on the phone, and it helped her feel connected. Another commented, "It occurs to me that the feeling of being in love that I've had at first with so many guys is actually nausea," and another added, "I need a lot of solitude in order to hear myself think."

We didn't all feel the same about being single, but we felt connected to each other and we made each other laugh.

It's hard work trying to meet a partner. It generally doesn't happen by itself if you're an older woman and so you have to take the initiative. People used to tell me, "Just let go and that's when it will happen," but I noticed they stopped saying it when

I got past sixty. You're constantly reaching for a state other than the one you're in, and this, as we know from Buddha and other experts, is the cause of suffering. Joy comes from accepting things as they are, but when you are looking for a mate, you are wishing for something you don't have.

I couldn't completely enjoy the fullness of my life because I always had this partner business in the back of my mind. It wasn't just the feeling of dissatisfaction that got me down; it was the constant strategizing, like making my vacation plans according to where I might meet the most single men. I was too old to sign up for hang-gliding lessons, but a wilderness photography class bore temporary fruit in the form of a dinner date. And then I was reminded again that there's a lot of distance to travel between meeting a guy and setting up house with him.

Sixty came and went and there was no new boyfriend.

I look back over my life and I wonder what my part is in all of this. Am I single due to dumb luck? karma? choice? statistics?

A familiar demon whispers in my ear that I am simply incapable of being in a committed relationship. A gentler voice suggests that I don't have a partner because I don't *want* one. Maybe *I'm* the one who has turned away from mating, without consciously admitting it, because I love my independence. Or a darker thought comes: maybe I've become attached to my loneliness; maybe loneliness is my significant other.

But lonely is a feeling, not a marital state. It's a simple feeling. It's clean and sad, and then it fades, and comes back later, and goes again. If I let myself feel the sadness when it comes, it loosens the bitterness of envy and regret. Bitterness is clenched, but sadness flows through it and melts it. Lonely turns into alone. I'm alive, alone.

Izumi Shikibu, a Japanese woman poet of the tenth century, wrote:

Watching the moon
at midnight,
solitary, mid-sky,
I knew myself completely,
no part left out.

Gradually, without noticing when it happened, I seem to have let go of trying. It's a big relief, I can tell you, not to be scanning the horizon for a spiritually minded socially engaged emotionally intelligent senior bachelor every time I leave the house. There are even days when I forget to look at the ring fingers of men my age when I first meet them.

I acknowledge that finding a partner can happen late in life, to straight people as well as gay people. It happened to Miss Punderson, after all. It might happen if you keep trying—especially if you're not too fussy—and it's remotely possible even if you stop trying. My widowed grandmother embarked on a happy second marriage when she was sixty-five, and two friends in my Zen community fell in love with each other in their seventies. I'm happy for them. I'll say it again: I'm happy for them.

I'm making it a practice now to refuse envy, and I do mean practice, because it doesn't come easy. When I notice envy's hot flicker, I think about the Buddhist quality of *mudita*, or sympathetic joy. Taking joy in the joy of others is the flip side of envy, and anyway, I probably wouldn't have been happy married to Norman Rockwell.

I'm turning my attention now to enjoying the life I have. I'm studying the benefits of being single.

A married Zen friend said, "You're lucky. You have opportunities I don't have to explore solitude. You can investigate what it means to be a human being."

This makes me think of Sumangalamata, the wife of a hat maker, who was one of Buddha's first women followers, in the sixth century BCE. She wrote the following poem:

At last free,
at last I am a woman free!
No more tied to the kitchen,
stained amid the stained pots,
no more bound to the husband
who thought me less
than the shade he wove with his hands.
No more anger, no more hunger,
I sit now in the shade of my own tree.
Meditating thus, I am happy, I am serene.

My friend reminds me: "Being married is like running a three-legged race, twenty-four seven. You have to compromise all the time. He likes two-percent milk; I prefer one-percent. He wants to arrive at the party on time; I want to get there half an hour late. He wants to set the clock radio; I want to sleep in. But you can do whatever you want. You can go wherever you want."

The poet May Sarton said, "Alone we can afford to be wholly whatever we are, and to feel whatever we feel absolutely. That is a great luxury!"

I should laminate these quotes and keep them ready in my wallet for the next time I stumble across one of those books about soul mates.

There's another good thing about being single, and it has to do with renunciation. Aging urges relinquishment upon me. It's time to scale back, to simplify my life. Everyone, whether single or double, finds out that getting old rhymes with letting go, but the go-letting of old-getting is easier to embrace if you're single. You can give away books and dishes without asking anyone.

Sometimes, not just when I'm lying awake at three o'clock in the morning, but at other times as well, I think of Peace Pilgrim. She walked back and forth across the United States from the time she was forty-four until her death at the age of seventy-three. She carried no money and had no possessions but the clothes she wore and a few things in her pockets. Her vow was to "remain a wanderer until mankind has learned the way of peace, walking until given shelter and fasting until given food." I couldn't do what she did—that was her way, not mine—but it makes me feel brave to think about her. She didn't have a husband either.

The main thing is, I'm not separate, I only think I am. I'm one of the jewel-like nodes in Indra's Net, that vast spiderweb of the universe. I'm not a thing at all, I'm an intersection where filaments connect. Pluck me out and the whole thing falls apart, like a knitted shawl unraveling from one dropped stitch. The universe holds me and the universe needs me. No way is the universe going to leave me for a younger woman.

I'm learning to meet my most intimate needs without a significant other now. I keep a long-handled bamboo backscratcher on my bedside table. I've named it "My Husband." It's like having my cake and eating it, too—I'm getting those hard-to-reach places between the shoulder blades scratched without having to pick up anyone else's socks.

My friend Walter was in his seventies when he left his apartment in San Francisco, where he was surrounded by doting friends and relatives, and moved into a tiny cottage at the edge of an apple orchard in Sonoma County, in search of more solitude. I was telling him about my struggle with loneliness, and he said he loved his own company. "I'll be taking a walk on the beach," he said, "and I'll say to myself: 'Hey Walter, ol' buddy! It's great to take a walk with you!'" He clapped himself affectionately on the shoulder. "You could do the same," he told me.

So sometimes, thinking of him, I call out to myself, "Hey, Sue, old pal!" and I clap myself on the shoulder, too, pretending to enjoy my own company as much as Walter enjoys his. It doesn't take away the sadness, but it helps.

# Exchanging Self and Other

Those desiring speedily to be
a refuge for themselves and others
should make the interchange of "I" and "other,"
and thus embrace a sacred mystery.

—Shantideva, *The Way of the Bodhisattva*

I'M LOOKING OVER my laptop out the window of a former bait shack turned summer cottage on the coast of Maine, where my old friend Susie and I are spending a week on vacation. It's late afternoon. I've paused in my writing, and I'm watching Susie take pictures of the fleshy boulders, with the water of Penobscot Bay lapping up into the cracks between them. She and her long shadow move lightly over the granite, stopping and going and stopping again, like a spider.

I first met Susie when she lived across the hall from me our freshman year of college at Radcliffe. She had come to New England from Mexico, where, as the daughter of a blacklisted Hollywood screenwriter, she had lived since the age of eight. I had come to college from two blocks away, where I had grown up, and so, like an armchair traveler, I was glad to make a friend who brought me the taste of worlds I had never imagined—Hollywood, Mexico City, American Communists. But even before I knew any of that about her, and I didn't know it right away because she was shy, I was drawn to her. You can fall in love with a person you want for a friend, without any romantic feeling, especially when you're a college freshman, wondering what kind of a person you are and what kind of person you want to be.

Susie wore her hair in a long brown braid that hung down her back, with a thick piece of Mexican yarn woven into it, sometimes a bright lime green, sometimes fuchsia. Another girl in our freshman dorm used to creep up behind Susie in the corridor and suddenly pull on her braid, calling out, "Ding dong! Ding dong!" Susie would mutter "Don't!" and scurry away. It made my scalp sting, too, when it happened.

We were roommates the next three years of college. I remember her climbing the walls at night in our shared room in the college dorm. Literally. I woke more than once to see her kneeling on her bed and clawing at the wall beside it, as if she were trying to climb up or out, and calling out in words I couldn't understand. When I woke her to reassure her, she didn't know where she was. We were a long way from Mexico City.

She took me to visit her family in the summer of 1962. They had moved from Mexico City to Italy. We were nineteen. Her parents, her five siblings, and various extended family and guests were spending the summer in a rented house perched at the top of a cliff on the Italian Riviera. We sat on a patio, under a grape arbor, looking over the dark turquoise sea, eating fresh croissants from the local bakery, and I listened eagerly to their talk, mostly in English but sometimes in Spanish, about LSD and psychoanalysis, and about ex-Communist friends back in Hollywood who were starting to work again under their own names. Susie's mother included me in the conversation, as if I were a grown-up, even though I didn't know what they were talking about most of the time.

Susie introduced me to faraway places and ideas. I, on the other hand, had a family up the street from our dorm, and so I could offer her a taste of home and the familiar ruckus of younger siblings. My parents grew fond of her, and sometimes she came for Sunday dinner. I think it helped her feel the ground under her feet to know a family who lived in an old house made of wood, with a fire in the living room fireplace on cold New England Sundays.

The year after we graduated from college, Susie became my first close friend to have a child. I went to see her and the baby in a tiny upstairs flat in Cambridge on a bright winter day, with snow on the streets and sun on the snow. I was excited. I wanted to know what motherhood was like. I don't remember anything Susie said, but I remember sunlight blazing through curtainless windows onto the creamy apartment walls, and the quick flick of a smile she gave me before her eyes went back to the baby. I remember how deeply she and her daughter, who was wrapped in a white flannel blanket, gazed at each other.

She sent me out to buy nursing pads so that the milk that was leaking from her breasts wouldn't soak through her shirt. I had never heard of nursing pads. I wondered: how does one learn about such things? I walked down the snowy streets to the drugstore, and back to the apartment, nursing pads in hand, feeling important and useful. Up the wooden stairs and into that nest of sleepy, milky light. So this was what new motherhood was like, this commanding brightness. That baby is now in her forties. She doesn't know it, but when I see her as a grown-up, as I occasionally do, she still shines for me—the first baby in my friendship circle.

After Susie and I were both divorced, we lived for a year in her house in Cambridge together, with our four young children, two hers and two mine. The kids formed a detective club called the Non-Squeaky Sneakers, and Susie took pictures of them climbing on fire escapes and spying through windows in the neighborhood, looking for suspicious clues. I wrote the text, and we made a book together.

When I moved to California, I didn't see her or even talk to her often, but our connection stayed strong over both time and space. We could always pick the thread right up, as if we'd been in the same room the whole time. When I was in a bad depression some years ago, there was a patch of time when I phoned her almost every day. She listened to me across the miles, and talked to me, and sent me homeopathic remedies.

As you grow older, old friends become more precious. Unlike family, friends start out by choosing each other, but if the friendship continues over time, through thick and thin, old friends become family. Old friends are a great benefit of growing old. I thought I had old friends when I was young, but I couldn't know then what an old friend was. After all, you can't have a friendship that's any older than you are, and the older you get, the older your friendships are.

In Muir Woods National Park in California, I have seen the cross section of a giant redwood tree, a thousand years old, with a ring for every year. An old friendship is like an old tree, with rings and rings of shared experiences under the outer bark, making the friendship thicker and taller. Sometimes, like a redwood tree, there may even be a burned out hollow part in the trunk, but the friendship still stands.

Childhood friends keep me connected to the whole narrative of my life. The further I get from my childhood, the harder it is to believe that I was once a nine-year-old girl practicing juggling with my best friend in her back yard until we could both do three crab apples, but my friend can confirm it. She was there. She was my witness and I was hers. In this way, I find as I get older that my life does not belong to me alone—it belongs to the people I've spent it with. My childhood belongs to my childhood friends, and theirs to me.

I recently visited that same friend after she had knee surgery. She lives far away from me, in the same house she grew up in, the house with the crab apple tree whose fruit we used for juggling, the house where she showed me how to put in a tampon, the house where we talked late into the night about Einstein's theory of relativity and how time passes at different speeds. More than fifty years later, when she showed me the scar on her knee, I had a powerful moment of recognition. I thought: I know that knee, with or without its scar. If somebody showed me that knee, and only that knee, through a peephole, I would know whose knee it was. It matters to me what happens to that familiar knee.

Near the end of his life, my father reconnected with people from his childhood and youth. I think it must have been after his sister died. He had always distanced himself from his privileged background and from the conservative values of the family he grew up in, so I was surprised when, as an old man, blind and sick with cancer, he took a bus to visit a cousin in Maine whom he hadn't seen for forty years, and he flew to California to see a long-lost friend from boarding school. It was a lot of trouble. He wept, telling me how much it meant to him to reconnect with them. He said they were the only people left who had known him as a child.

Here's what I mean when I say old friends stick by each other through thick and thin. One time, I hired a professional organizer to help me sort the papers in my study, a task that always makes me tremble. We went through old files together and filled many grocery bags and cardboard cartons with paper to be recycled. She showed me a whole new system for dealing with my incoming mail—"Verticalize! Verticalize!" was her refrain—and she gave me a list of office supplies to put the system into place. I walked her out the front door and said good-bye.

On my way back into the house, I picked up a big pile of mail from my mailbox and carried it into the study. I didn't know where to put it—my system was in transition. And suddenly, I totally lost it. I had what I think was the only temper tantrum I've ever had. Screaming "I hate this!" at the top of my lungs, I kicked violently at each bag and box of papers, upending them. I hurled armfuls of papers into the air, making a blizzard, until the floor of my study was covered in drifts of paper, and then, exhausted, I sat down in the middle and cried. How would I ever get out of this?

Then a ray of light came into my mind. It was the thought of a friend, a friend who lives nearby and works at home, a friend I'd known long enough that I was pretty sure he'd still love me even after he found out what I'd done. I called him up and said I needed him. Luckily, he had an hour before his next piano student was to arrive, and he came right over. He was impressed by the chaos but not afraid of it—they weren't *his* papers. He appreciated my vigor, and he pointed out that my tantrum was well-planned, since all of the paper was on the way out anyway. I'd had all the fun of making a mess without doing any damage. He got me laughing, and together we put the paper back in the paper bags, and together we put it out to be recycled.    ✓

Friends see each other through changes. For years I've been taking a walk with a friend every Thursday morning. When we were young single mothers, we used to take our children skiing together. We also hiked together. Later, on our weekly walks, we took a trail in the hills behind Berkeley. The walks became shorter when we stopped doing the very steep part at the top because of my knees. The next change was to a gentler but still sloping walk in a pretty park near her office—well, actually it's a cemetery, but we don't lie down in it. Lately my friend has been having trouble with her hip, and so we have further adjusted our walk, staying on level ground, in the early morning streets of our neighborhood. On our last walking date, she arrived at the appointed time to pick me up, but she had just done something to her back while getting into the car, and so for our walk time she lay on her back on my living room floor and I brought her a cold pack from the fridge. I sat in the rocking chair beside her, and we talked until she had to drive to work.

I'm noticing that when someone you love needs help, it feels good to give it. In order to be "a refuge for myself and others," as Shantideva says, I try to "make the interchange of 'I' and 'other,'" to remember that helping a friend is not so different from receiving help from a friend, and this gives me confidence that my friends are glad to help me when I need them. There are plenty of opportunities going both directions.

✓ The older you get, the more your friends have health problems. A close friend was seriously ill a couple of years ago with a rare form of viral pneumonia. Many years before, soon after I moved to California, she had been the one to introduce me to the high country of Yosemite. When I got short of breath hiking up the trail behind her, in air thinner than I'd ever breathed before, she encouraged me: slow and steady wins the race, she said. She told me to breathe from deep in my belly, with my diaphragm.

When she got sick, I sat with her often during her prolonged hospital stay. These hours had not been planned for in my busy schedule, and yet there was time to be with her. It was not a problem. Wholeheartedness led the way, and it felt good not to question, not to hedge, not to hold back. It was my turn to encourage her to breathe.

I know a woman in her seventies who has formed what she calls a "pod" with a few old and trusted friends. They have made a pact to go to each other when the need arises, to "be there for each other." She says this might mean sitting by a bedside, advocating in the hospital, or holding hands when something terrible happens. It might even mean helping each other die. It might mean saying, "The state in which I see you now is what you always told me you didn't want."

I've been thinking about it. You could make such an agreement explicit, like a wedding vow. *If you need me, I will do everything in my power to come to you. If I need you, I will expect the same of you.* You could say it out loud, or you could even write up a document.

And even without saying anything, I'm in a sort of pod with my friends.

Old friendships are a benefit of getting old, but old friends also die. It's lonely when you're very old and your close friends are gone. This was impressed upon me when I visited my grandmother's beloved lifetime friend, "Aunt Dorothy," several years after my grandmother's death. She was about ninety, and tiny, sitting up in her bed at home, like a little hill in the bedclothes, a small bump of life sticking up above the plain, all her friends gone. She told me she missed my grandmother every single day of her life. She said she didn't want to be alive any more now that there was no one left in her generation. I guess the silver lining of having your friends all die before you is that it helps you feel more ready to die. I'm thinking of the old spiritual "Swing Low, Sweet Chariot": "If you get there before I do, tell all my friends I'm coming, too."

Now, over forty years after we first met, Susie and I have come to this bait shack at the edge of the harbor, to take pictures and write. We are practicing the exchange of self and other. Susie comes from California and lives in Massachusetts, and I come from Massachusetts and live in California. She, the photographer, has lately become a writer, and I am learning to take pictures. Perhaps our next collaborative project will be a book with text by her and photos by me.

This week I read a piece of the young adult novel she's working on and gave her feedback, and yesterday she taught me how to get greater depth of field, so that both the green seaweed floating on the surface and the barnacled rocks under the water were in focus. I love that phrase, *depth of field*. It describes our friendship.

Out the window the low sun paints the rocks with yellow light and moving shadows, so that figure and ground keep changing, and the rocks flow into each other, soft as water. Now Susie stands with one foot on either side of a crevice, in her familiar bow-legged stance. She points the camera down, adjusts the focus, pauses, completely still. She's waiting for something, maybe a wave to lap up. I hope she gets just the shot she wants. I feel indescribably fond of her, in her black wool cap.

We have the same name. In college we were both called Susie. Once, she woke me up in our dorm room, calling, "Susie!"

"Yes?" I said.

"Oh my god!" she said. "That was so weird! When I called you Susie just then I meant *me*."

# House of Commons

OVER TIME, without my planning it, my house has become part of the commons.

I've lived in the same house for close to forty years, almost unheard of in this age of family uprootings. I've always shared the house with other people, and I still do.

The first epoch in the house was the time of my children's growing up. In 1972, I was a newly divorced mother of two small children, and I bought the house in Berkeley, California, with the help of my parents. I was afraid I'd feel isolated if I lived alone with the kids, especially since their father moved away soon after we parted. I thought it would be good for them, too, to have other caring adults in the household. I chose a homey, shingled house, whose four-plus bedrooms made it plenty big enough to share with others. Two venerable walnut trees arched over the house in the back yard.

Friends moved in with me—and we four adults and three kids lived together for the first few years. The walnut trees bore many walnuts that we dried in the attic and put into pies. The other mother and I took turns making supper for the kids. A housemate painted a sun on the kitchen ceiling, with wiggly yellow rays reaching out.

We had massage classes on the living room floor in front of the fire, and wild parties with homemade music. I see now that it might not have been the most stable household possible for my children, but in Berkeley in the seventies, it seemed almost normal. We were transcending the claustrophobic limits of the nuclear family.

The time went by, the people came and went. Those who moved in were always friends or friends of friends. An artist slept in the kitchen hallway in order to use her bedroom for a studio. One man spent hours in his room practicing reflexology on his own feet while wearing a turban and pantaloons. As the tides ebbed and flowed, bringing Zen practitioners, boyfriends, exchange students, dogs and cats, the kids and I remained onshore.

People who didn't live in the house came to know it, too. The massage classes gave way to more sober events, like monthly letter-writing parties for political causes. There were house meetings about the war in El Salvador and fundraising potlucks for the nuclear freeze campaign. The kids and their friends played music in the house on various instruments. For years, three friends and I, with the help of our several children, produced a family humor magazine—*Garlic, the Breath of the People*—on the dining room table, pasting down the drawings and typewritten columns with wax and getting it ready for the printer. We had three hundred subscribers.

The house grew its own homey culture, like yogurt or sourdough starter. If you spilled something on the comfortable, slightly shabby furniture it didn't matter much. There was usually something that needed fixing—a leaky faucet, or a broken step on the back porch—but the house had a mood of friendly welcome.

Many housemates sat at the kitchen table with me. They stayed a year, or two, or three, and eventually moved on. When my children, too, flew the coop, the house seemed to lose its purpose. All those years, living with other people, I had been making a home for my children, and so it had been my home, too.

Now it felt big and echoey, not like home. Still, it was home base, if not home, and I stayed on. A college friend from Senegal and his school-age sons lived with me for a year while he taught at the university. A couple, friends of a friend, arrived from Vermont in a gypsy wagon they had built, and stayed for a few years, to be near their Berkeley granddaughter. And my sons came back for visits, sometimes long ones.

I was continually learning the lesson of impermanence. I knew that some of the housemates would be leaving from the moment they arrived, like the friend from Africa who had a yearlong appointment. Occasionally I asked someone to leave. But there were some I wished would stay.

Still, I understood that I was the owner. I couldn't have my cake and eat it, too; I couldn't expect people to stay in my house exactly as long as I wanted them to and no longer. So the house was a lopsided community, privately owned. At one point I almost persuaded dear friends to buy half the house, but it turned out there were tax impediments.

When I'd been in the house for twenty-five years, I had a reunion party, of all the people I could find who had lived there with me. The ones who were living in Chicago, Prince Edward Island, Denmark, Germany, France, and Senegal didn't come, but local people came, and we sat in a big circle in the living room and told stories: about the time my dog ate a housemate's lump of hashish and collapsed on the front steps with a piece of it still on her tongue that he managed to salvage, about the comparative croissant tasting event, the visiting teenagers from the Soviet Union, and the time one of my kids, at the age of five, cut up a housemate's diaphragm with scissors. To have all those people sitting together in the living room at the same time, to have twenty-five years of household history crunched together in one moment, was both wonderful and sad. Was it me or the house itself who had gathered us all in? And why, when so many people had passed through, did I alone remain?

I was glad when my sister and her two daughters moved in with me, but when she bought her own house two years later and they moved out, it seemed like the end of an era. I thought it was time for me to go, too.

In 2000, I rented out the house and set off to explore other possibilities. I lived in a wine barrel in a retreat center in the country, but it was too small; I rented a room in someone else's house, but it didn't feel like my community; I rented a beautiful flat by the beach, but it was a long haul to get to my job and my friends in Berkeley, and I was lonesome. After a few years, I decided to move back in.

I'm still here, still sharing the house with others.

It's hard work taking care of an old house, endlessly fixing and painting. It takes time, money, and energy. I'm in my mid-sixties. When I moved in, I was twenty-nine. I'm able to cope with it now, but for how much longer?

I think about my contemporaries, my friends and relatives: almost every one of them lives either alone or with a partner (unless they are temporarily living with me), except for a few who live in residential Zen communities. How odd that I'm the only one still living in shared housing, like a throwback. It's not a policy decision; I'm certainly not defying the bourgeois lifestyle. Life would be so much simpler if I sold the house and moved into a little apartment or a condo.

But here's the thing: I don't want to live alone. I need my own private space, but I like to hear the sounds of people I love knocking around the house. I like to smell their coffee in the morning (I don't drink coffee anymore), and I like to sit down to a meal together, not every evening, but often, and find out what's shaking.

What does an older single woman do if she doesn't want to live alone? I could sell my house and move into a cohousing community with strangers. I could move into a Zen community, if I were willing to get up at 4:30 every morning and dedicate my days to a demanding practice schedule. I could join with friends to plan a community together, but when a group of us tried that years ago, nobody ever stepped forward to do the full-time work of finding the place and setting it up, and the group fell apart. If the community already existed, if my dearest friends lived in a homey, socially relevant, spiritually grounded community in the country close to Berkeley, with a good view of an unpolluted body of water, with shared vegetarian meals twice a week, and room for visiting grandchildren, I'd move right in. But I'm not holding my breath.

There's "retirement living." My mother and stepfather lived happily in an apartment building for seniors for the last fifteen years of their lives. But they were older then than I am now, and I'm not ready for that yet.

Community exists through time, not just in space. By now the house itself has become a member of my extended family. When friends or relatives strain their backs, they let themselves into the yard through the gate and get into the hot tub. They celebrate birthdays and anniversaries in the back yard. My grown sons, my daughter-in-law, my granddaughter, my nieces and nephews come visiting. The house is a way station for friends in transition. It's become part of the commons, and I'm currently its steward. Others, through use, have gained a right of way. I don't quite feel I have the right to sell it, not yet. I keep it open as a place of possibility. The painted sun is still shining on the kitchen ceiling.

In recent years, like chickens coming home to roost, people who lived in the house before have returned. My sister recently cycled through a second time, and a young woman who lived here as a child turned up briefly. Now a niece lives in the house with me, and I'm waiting to see who else is coming.

I know the time is approaching when I'll quit being the housemother, and I don't mean by dying. I'll get too tired to figur out what to do about the muddy basement, or I'll get too sad when someone I love moves out. A change is coming. Maybe someone will move in with me and promise never to leave, or someone will invite me to live with them. Maybe I'll divide the house into two apartments and rent or sell one of them to a friend. Maybe I'll be ready for a retirement community, or surprise myself by wanting solitude.

It's not going to be an easy transition. I'll need courage. But the commons is a living, breathing organism that stretches beyond the walls of my house. I'm part of it, and these days I have faith that the commons will take care of me in ways I can't foresee.

# Getting Good at Staying Still

I was having Cheerios and milk with my mother at the little table beside the window, in her retirement building in Chicago. Her sixth-floor apartment overlooked Lake Michigan, and it was one of my mother's greatest pleasures in life to sit in her favorite chair and watch the passing of ore boats and clouds. This was the first morning of my visit, and my mother turned her attention from her lake to her daughter, saying, "Your hair is so wild! Can't you do something to get it out of your face?"

"Why don't you ever tell me when you *like* my hair?" I said.

She tried to redeem herself that evening, lavishing compliments upon me when I put barrettes in my hair before we went downstairs to dinner. But the next morning, again, she looked at me over her bowl of cereal, with her head cocked, and I felt it coming.

"You looked so beautiful last night," she said, trying to be diplomatic. "I could hardly take my eyes off you." I knew that was just the prelude. "But this morning . . . can't you just brush it back?"

"Mom," I said, "I'm sixty-three years old. I'm too old for you to be telling me how to wear my hair." Apparently I wasn't too old to mind.

"I just want you to know how nice it looks when you brush it back."

"I know how you like it, Mom."

"No, you don't! That's why I'm telling you."

I thought: *You've been talking to me about my hair for sixty years. Do you think I don't know what pleases you?* But I didn't say it out loud.

Anyway, I wasn't in an entirely blameless position myself. A couple of years before, when my mother's hair had been down to her shoulders and she sometimes wore it in pigtails, she asked me if I liked it that way. I said I didn't think it was "age appropriate." (If she hadn't been my mother, I probably would have been charmed by her braids.) She pretended she thought that was a great witticism on my part, and a couple of times I heard her say to friends, "Susan thinks my braids are not 'age appropriate'!" But it hurt her feelings. Not long after, she cut her hair short, so that it floated soft and white around her face. And did I mention to her the next time I saw her how nice her hair looked? No, not until she asked me outright whether I thought her new haircut was age appropriate.

My mother was a generous woman, and she loved her children and grandchildren with unconditional love—almost. As the Zen teacher Suzuki Roshi said to his students as he was trying to explain Buddha nature: "You're all perfect exactly as you are, *and* you could use a little improvement."

I rented a car for my weeklong visit, so that I could take my mother places. She had given up driving a couple of years before, after she drove into a parked car for no particular reason. It was hard for her—not driving. And she couldn't walk far because of her bad back, so the bus stop two blocks away was beyond her reach. A van from the building took residents shopping, but walking around the enormous supermarket, even with a shopping cart to lean on, was hard work for her. And she hated not being able to choose when to go.

I did errands for her: I was glad to be able to take her to the eye doctor to get her cataracts looked at. Doctors' appointments were an emotional issue for her, and the older she got the more of them there were. In a phone conversation not long before my visit she had spoken to me enviously of a friend in her retirement building. "Janet's daughter drives her to *every* doctor's appointment. Oh, I *wish* one of you lived in Chicago!" My siblings and I tried to coordinate our visits with her doctors' appointments, but we all lived far away and couldn't be counted on on a regular basis. She went to most of them by taxi, and it was a long wait for a taxi.

One day that week I took her to an exhibit of Japanese prints at the Art Institute and pushed her through the galleries in the folding wheelchair she used for such excursions. Several times, when she wanted to look at a different picture than the one I was aiming for, she quite literally put her foot down, and suddenly the wheelchair wouldn't go, like a locked shopping cart. It was annoying until I looked at it from her point of view and realized it was her way of reclaiming a little control over her own experience.

I tried to be helpful in other ways as well. My mother's culinary needs were simple; the system in her building was that she ate her dinners downstairs in the community dining room and prepared her own breakfasts and lunches, which were minimal, in her tiny kitchen. So I cleaned out her refrigerator, bought cold cereals and little yogurts, and made a big pot of leek and potato soup and put some of it away in the freezer for future lunches.

Then there was her computer. I showed her a couple of things she always forgot between visits: how to change the margins in her word-processing program and how to send an e-mail. This was rewarding for me, because my mother was the only person in the world who considered me a computer expert.

I admired my mother's life. Chicago was her city; she had grown up there. She still had old friends outside of the building whom she saw now and then, and she had a rich life inside the building. This time I visited the weekly poetry class she had been leading there for many years. One of the residents, a descendant of the African American poet Paul Laurence Dunbar, brought several editions of his books to the class, and the assembled group, a mix of whites and African Americans, had a challenging discussion about writing in African American vernacular English. I was impressed. I could almost imagine myself in a group like this.

But I would have hated to be as cooped up as my mother was. Sometimes she didn't leave the building for days and she only knew the temperature outside by how the people who were walking their dogs along the lakefront were dressed. She spent hours at her post by the window, swiveling her chair through the 180-degree range of her view, looking out at the ducks on the lake through her binoculars. As a matter of fact, I think she preferred to *look* at the weather—whatever it was—from her comfortable chair than to be out in it. I got restless in the small apartment, in spite of my years of Buddhist practice, but my mother, having to stay put, was getting good at staying still.

The day before I went back to California, it was snowing when I woke up. I slipped out of the apartment while my mother was still asleep. I took the pedestrian tunnel under the outer drive and walked in the little park on the lakefront that was right across from her building. There was no one else there; mine were the first footprints in the fresh snow. I could have been in the country, with the little white peaks on top of the fence posts, and the lake beside me that had no end because the falling snow blocked out the smokestacks of Indiana, and the squirrels dropping things from the branches. I could have been in the country except for the roar of traffic behind me. I thought: *I'll visit her when it's spring, when the snow is gone and the sun is out, and I'll push her in her wheelchair through the park, so she'll be able to hear the birds and smell the willows.*

I turned to walk back and saw my mother's building, on the other side of the river of cars. I counted up six floors to pick out her window in the brick façade, and waved, just in case she'd gotten up and happened to be looking out.

That evening, my last, my mother had a party before dinner for a group of friends she called "the mothers of daughters." All of the women had faraway daughters who visited them there—like me, from Berkeley, California. Before the party, I brushed my hair and clipped it back as neatly as I could.

Six women traveled by elevator to my mother's apartment for wine and those little goldfish-shaped crackers. I didn't have to take their coats when they arrived, because they had all come from inside the building, but I took two walkers and put them aside. My mother was happy to see them—she always said she liked to show off her children to her friends. They settled in a semicircle facing the big window. The day's light was fading to gray over the lake, and the snow was already dirty at the edge of the road below.

The only woman I hadn't met before said: "You look just like your mother!" Even in old age my mother was an attractive woman, but does any daughter want to be told she looks just like her mother? It wasn't so much that I minded if there was a resemblance, but I did want to look *younger* than my mother. In fact, whenever I had occasion to ride in the elevator of her building without her, I had a horror of being mistaken for one of the residents. I was almost sixty-five—officially old enough to live there.

I was moved by this group of women—all of them lively and warm-hearted, all of them dealing with the ruinations of old age. Betty, the oldest of the group, was in her nineties. The others were all in their eighties. Betty was robust and always laughing. A few years before, she and my mother had ridden the trans-Siberian railroad together, but after that she had begun to suffer from dizzy spells and had had to give up traveling. One of the guests couldn't hear a thing, and another, whether she was sitting or standing, was bent into the letter C.

Jane, who had been my mother's friend since childhood, had advanced mouth cancer. She had lost her teeth and had an artificial palate. She didn't go down to the dining room for dinner because, as she told my mother, she was afraid it would spoil her tablemates' appetites to see her eating. It even hurt to talk, and her speech was slightly impaired, but she was a woman of remarkable fortitude, and she still joined in the conversation. When it turned to the popular topic of visits from adult children, she remarked wryly, "A son is a son till he gets him a wife, but a daughter's a daughter the rest of her life."

All of these women were widows, including my mother. I couldn't know how hard it was to become a widow after sharing your life with another person for fifty years. Nor could I know what a relief it might be, after the last long years of caretaking.

When you look at old women from the outside, not identifying with them, you don't think how lonely they might be, or how much patience it takes to get the walker in and out of the elevator. You forget that they didn't used to be like that, that they used to go canoeing in the Minnesota woods or waltz until the wee hours, that they knew another kind of life outside this building. You think they came into the world wrinkled and deaf.

I passed the crackers, like a good daughter. I offered wine, red or white, in my mother's pretty blue Mexican glasses. Her youthful cat, Sigo (for "Significant Other": my mother adopted her after my stepfather died), lay on her back and pawed the air, wanting to be played with. My mother held a wire with a fluff ball on the end and dangled it in front of Sigo, who hunkered down, moving nothing but the tip of her tail, and then leapt straight up so suddenly that we all laughed.

Betty said to me, "I hear you were just on a long Zen meditation retreat. Did it make you calm?"

As a Buddhist convert, I was slightly exotic there. That afternoon my mother had introduced me to two of her fellow residents in the elevator, where a lot of her social interactions took place. "This is my Buddhist daughter from California!" she had said proudly. They wanted to know all about Buddhism, and whether or not I believed in reincarnation, but I didn't really have time to explain between the sixth floor and the first.

Now I responded to Betty's question. "You're not supposed to try to accomplish anything at all, not even calmness," I said. "The idea is to let go of gaining mind. Let go of your attachments."

"Well, I can see that *I* don't need Zen meditation," said Betty. "Getting old forces you to let go of one damn thing after another!" The others laughed in agreement.

"I like Zen," my mother said, "because it says you should be in the present. That's important in old age. I'm losing interest in my past—it was so long ago! And it's pointless to think about the future—what future? But the present! There's plenty going on right now, I tell myself."

I offered more wine, but there was only one taker, and I wondered if they had always practiced such moderation. The conversation moved on to the new cook in the kitchen downstairs and a dangerously creamy mushroom sauce he had used on the chicken. As the women talked and laughed, as they passed around the bowl of crackers with shaky hands, I studied them. I saw how they paid attention to each other. They were accomplished people: scholars, artists, social workers, poets, raisers of families. Now in old age, they were accomplishing friendship, accomplishing community.

My mother was only twenty years ahead of me, and at the rate things were going, I would be her age in no time. She was scouting the territory for me, and it behooved me to observe carefully.

It was 5:30 P.M.—time, in that establishment, to go down to dinner. After I fetched the two walkers from the corner of the room, the seven mothers of daughters and the one daughter—me—started down the long hall to the elevator.

My mother rode in her wheelchair, making it go by walking her feet along the floor in front of her, like a toddler on a riding toy. This was how she liked to do it when she was on her home turf. She said she got her best exercise in her wheelchair. People assumed she was in a wheelchair because her legs didn't work, but it was her back that hurt if she walked more than about fifty paces.

Sometimes, on a good back day, she walked to the elevator with a cane. Her cane had a handle that flipped down sideways and became a tiny seat, allowing her to stop and rest. She ordered those canes from England. If you were looking at her from the front and she was sitting on her cane, it was startling, because you couldn't see the cane and she appeared to be doing a strenuous yoga posture—her knees partly bent, pretending to sit in a chair that wasn't there. But today was a wheelchair day.

Our ragtag band moved down the corridor, and I had to make a conscious effort to go slow. Betty, walking beside me, said, "You have such beautiful hair, Susan." My mother looked up at me from her wheelchair and we grinned at each other.

# Grandmother Mind

WHEN MY SON NOAH was about four and I was a harried single mother, he told me he wasn't going to have children. It was time for me to take him to nursery school, and he refused to wear anything but his Superman costume, which was in the washing machine, clean but wet. I exploded in irritation, and he announced, "I'm *never* going to have kids. It's too much trouble!"

I was chastened. "It's worth it, sweetie," I said. "It's definitely worth it!"

As he grew up, I watched him cuddle pets and babies, but he held to the plan of not having children into adulthood. My younger son, Sandy, likes kids but is presently single, and I was beginning to fear I might never become a grandmother. A person can take certain actions to make it more likely that she'll become a parent, but there's not much a person can do to produce grandchildren. So even when Noah got married, I tried to keep my mouth shut. I reminded myself that he didn't come into the world for the express purpose of giving me grandchildren. It was his and Arcelia's business. They had their careers to think of, along with the economic challenge of parenting, and concerns about the imperiled planet. Still, I did mention that I would be glad to babysit.

I was well loved by both of my grandmothers, in their different ways. "Grandma" took me to Quaker meeting, wrote out her favorite prayers for me in a little notebook, and took me down the lane to her sculpture studio, where she gave me clay to play with while she sculpted. I was her first grandchild, and when I climbed into bed with her in the morning, she'd take off the strange black sleep mask that made her look like the Lone Ranger and hang it on the bedpost. She'd reach out to me and I'd curl up beside her, loving the feel of the cool soft flesh that hung from her upper arms, and she'd say, "Good morning, my number one grandchild!"

My other grandmother, known as "Ma," kept lemon drops in a white glass chicken on her dresser, and if you wanted one all you had to do was cough a little fake cough and she'd say, "My dear, you must have something for your throat." Whenever we children visited, there were fresh-baked chocolate cupcakes with vanilla frosting on a blue tin plate in the kitchen, and you were allowed to help yourself whenever you wanted to. She always smelled delicious, of a certain perfume that nobody else ever smelled of, and she wore a gold chain bracelet with a tiny gold airplane dangling from it. I asked her why, and she told me it was a replica of the air force plane her youngest son, my uncle Morton, was piloting when he was shot down over Japan, and she wore it so she would never forget his courage. It had the exact serial number engraved on the wing, so small you couldn't even read it.

I learned from my grandparents the amazing truth that my own parents had been children long ago—I was stunned to learn, for example, that my father had been shy, that my mother had been mischievous. They weren't that way with me! I learned that sad things happen in people's lives, and they keep going. I learned of the turning of the generations: children turn into parents, and parents grow old and turn into grandparents. Grandparents change a still shot into a movie.

———

   · I was at home in Berkeley when Noah called me on a Sunday afternoon, from San Antonio, Texas, to tell me that his daughter had arrived. His voice was like a bowl of water he was trying not to spill. Paloma was twenty minutes old at the time, and they were still in the delivery room. Everybody was doing well. "Are you happy to be a grandma?" he asked eagerly, even though he knew the answer.

   "Are you kidding?! Nothing could make me happier!" Then I heard Paloma crying in the background. She wasn't exactly crying for joy, as I was; she was crying, Noah said, because they were sticking a needle in her heel to get some blood for a bilirubin test, and she didn't like it.

   Driving around Berkeley that afternoon, doing errands, alone in the car, I kept shouting out, "Paloma! Paloma!"

   · I thought of all the other babies born that day, all over the world, so many of them born into war, or crushing poverty. I have since learned, from Google, that there are about 353,000 births a day on Planet Earth. I guess you could say that all the babies born on the day I became a grandmother are my grandchildren.

   On that particular day, the front page of the *New York Times* told of civilian casualties in Beirut resulting from Israel's bombing of Hezbollah. I found myself wanting to propitiate the gods, God, the Universe, whatever—to thank them for Paloma's safe arrival and ask them to keep her and all babies safe. What offering could I make, and to whom? Checking my e-mail that birthday afternoon, I found a request for help from the Middle East Children's Alliance, and I made a donation in Paloma's name. A small gesture, standing for the juxtaposition it was part of my job, as a grandmother, to keep in mind: Paloma and all the others.

   When I arrived in San Antonio, Paloma was two weeks old. She was asleep on her back when Noah brought me into the house from the airport, so I could see her whole face. (Nowadays they tell parents always to put babies down to sleep on their backs, because of SIDS. This was new to me.) Right away I saw how much Paloma looks like Noah when he was a baby—defined, not blobby, her whole self already present in her face. And I saw that she has her mother's huge eyes. Soon she woke, and Arcelia nursed her, and then I held her against my chest.

I stayed for a week, in the hot Texas summer, leaving the house only twice to go to the grocery store in the mall. I did a lot of cooking while the family napped. I danced around the living room with Paloma, trying to soothe her when she was fussy by swinging her in my arms and singing to her. The more vigorously I jiggled her, the better she liked it, and she didn't care when I couldn't remember all the words to the songs I dragged up from the basement of my mind—Christmas carols and old Beatles songs. When she fell asleep in my arms, I lay down on my back on the couch, holding her carefully against my chest, and I let her sleep on top of my heart for as long as she cared to. In that time out of time, in that air-conditioned suburban living room, I smelled her sweet head and watched the oak leaves shifting in the hot breeze out the window.

I learned new things about taking care of babies—unfamiliar to me, but based on ancient wisdom. I learned about the five S's for soothing fussy babies: swaddling, swinging, letting them suck, holding them sideways, and making shushing noises. Noah was particularly good at the swaddling, and would coo to Paloma in a deep voice—"There, there, Pumpkin Head, now you're all cozy"—as he tucked the blanket corners around her arms and wrapped her into a snug little package. During the course of my visit I also heard her addressed, by both parents, in torrents of affection, as Petunia, Little Miss Piglet, Florecita, Sweet Pea, Calabacita, and even Bunion Cake.

As for me, to my great delight, Arcelia called me "Abuelita."

Sometimes I carried Paloma out into the back yard, even though it was 102 degrees. She instantly quieted. She looked up at the trees and the big space of sky, and I could see her feeling the *un*conditioned air on her cheeks. I could see she knew things were different here, in the big outdoors. Noah, too, had loved to look at leaves when he was a baby.

Zen Master Dogen, founder of the Soto School of Zen in Japan, had a student who was a sincere and disciplined monk, but he had one weakness—he did not have "grandmother mind." Dogen told him, "You can understand all of Buddhism, but you cannot go beyond your abilities and your intelligence unless you have *robai-shin*, grandmother mind, the mind of great compassion. This compassion must help all of humanity. You should not think only of yourself."

You don't need to be a grandmother to have grandmother mind. You can even be a celibate monk in a monastery.

Parents have to have a different kind of mind than grandparents. Parents have to attend to the nuts and bolts of their children's needs—feeding them, sheltering them, keeping them warm. They have to protect them from cars, from too much sugar, from kidnapping. Parents take care of the foreground. But grandmothers—both literal and metaphorical—can pay attention to the background, to the water and the air. We can tell the babies stories about the stars.

Sometimes, grandmothers have to take the place of parents. Sometimes the parents are in prison, or are children themselves, or they have died of AIDS. Sometimes their ability to take care of their children has been destroyed by warfare, homelessness, addiction. More and more grandmothers are heads of household, heroically raising their grandchildren in circumstances that don't leave them much time to waltz the babies around the house singing "Norwegian Wood." I want to keep all those other grandmothers in mind.

One day in San Antonio, I rose, made tea, and brought the *New York Times* in from the doorstep, while the rest of the family were having their morning nap. A front-page story about the bombing of Beirut was continued inside—I turned the page and suddenly there was a photograph of an infant half buried in rubble, her face coated with dust, a small hand showing between broken boards. I closed the paper and put it back on the table.

Later, when Noah sat down with his bowl of granola, I saw him open the paper to the same photo. I saw his eyes looking at that dead baby in the broken concrete and I heard him make a low groan in the back of his throat as he closed the paper even faster than I had done. It was harder for me to see him see the picture than it had been to look at it myself. I'm still a mother, as well as a grandmother. We didn't speak of it.

But, looking at Noah looking at Paloma—that was quite another matter. Arcelia told me the experts say you're *supposed* to gaze into a newborn's eyes in order to promote its healthy emotional development, but it was obvious that when Paloma's parents gazed into her eyes they weren't just following directions from a book.

To see your child happy to be a parent affirms the whole spiraling project—our ancestors coming down from the trees so long ago, and the babies staring back up into the branches.

Noah, the "too-much-trouble-to-have-kids" boy, is a dad. It *is* a lot of trouble, he's right about that. It's trouble getting up in the middle of the night, it's trouble doing all that laundry, it's trouble working to make the planet a safe place for children. It's trouble, but not too much.

It was hard to tear myself away at the end of the week. Noah put my bag in the trunk and we got in the car. Arcelia stood in the doorway with Paloma in her arms. As Noah backed the car out of the garage into the blazing Texas sun, Arcelia picked up Paloma's hand and waved it for her. "Good-bye, Abuelita!" Arcelia called.

"Good bye, Calabacita, little pumpkin," I answered.

# What If I Never Have Sex Again?

I MAY NEVER have sex again. May never lie spoon to spoon with another person. I don't feel like having sex right this minute, which is fortunate because I don't have anybody to have it with. But I'm not sure I'll keep on not wanting to have sex right this minute for the rest of my life. When I was younger and didn't have a partner I didn't think, "What if I never have sex again?" I assumed I was in between relationships. Now, in my mid-sixties, I wonder if I have quietly passed beyond "in between."

Even if I did want to have sex, maybe nobody would want to have sex with me. Confidence ebbs away as skin sags in private as well as public places. I suppose you could always resort to the cover of darkness, or never taking off your nightie, but can't fingers still feel the sag? Couples who grow old together get used to each other's sagging in slow increments, but it's a whole other matter to get to know somebody new when you're already wrinkled up. Plus, I'm not as bendable as I used to be.

I used to like sex a lot if I liked the person, but when I didn't have it, I didn't miss it much. Sometimes I missed the person. Saying I miss sex is like saying I miss wearing my hiking boots, when what I miss is standing at Paiute Pass watching the cloud shadows run across the lake below. I miss going where the hiking boots take me. "Having sex" isn't something that I can miss, all by itself, because I could never peel it away from the person who, moments before, might have been reading aloud to me in bed, and who, shortly afterward, might be snoring beside me just loud enough that I nudge him to quiet him.

Not having rolled in the hay for a while now—never mind exactly how long—I hardly ever think about it. I'm lucky not to want what I don't have. It's convenient. I want, as in *lack*, sex, but I don't want, as in *desire*, it. At the movies, in the erotic parts, I'm like an eight-year-old: "Oh gross! Hurry up and finish this scene! It has nothing to do with me!"

I used to be just plain interested in the whole subject of sex, and I liked writing about it, too. Now I prefer writing about not having sex.

I get annoyed with the way people are always saying, out of political correctness, that old people are sexy, too, that old folks can have rich sex lives, etc., etc. Yeah, but do we *have* to? Whatever old people want to do in bed is fine with me, but I don't want to feel like there's something wrong with me if I'm not doing it, too. I claim the right to lose libido as I get older. (Still, I'm not promising.)

I suspect that more people share my lack of desire than admit it. In the 1940s, Alfred Kinsey discovered that quite a few people were up to all kinds of tricks they had not been admitting, but now, post-Kinsey, post–sexual revolution, it's hard for people to admit what they're *not* doing.

I do miss some of the side effects of sex. You get to touch and be touched by another warm-blooded being. There are other ways to accomplish this: getting a massage and going to the dentist are two of the most expensive. Grandchildren provide cuddling for free, but my granddaughter lives more than a thousand miles away.

There are also pets. When I went on a solitary retreat in the woods, I took my sister's dog, Satchmo, with me for company. His fur felt good under my fingers. I groomed him with a curry brush every morning when we came back from our walk, to get the burrs out of his coat. Each time he saw me pick up the brush, he would come right to me and lean his body into mine. Sometimes he licked my face as I was brushing him, and I took it to mean, "Thank you. I love you." I missed his hugs and kisses when I returned him to my sister.

It feels like I sometimes go for as long as six months, the length of time between my dental hygienist appointments, without being touched by another human being. It's not really so, because I hug people in greeting, but those hugs don't last nearly as long as having my teeth cleaned.

Then there's the matter of intimacy, one of the most famous side effects of sex. Some would even say that sex is a side effect of intimacy. In any case, sex is an excellent way to blur the distinction between your innermost self and someone else's— probably the best. I've heard it said that sex is for making babies, but there are other ways of doing that nowadays; I think sex was invented for the very purpose of enabling us to discover that we are not separate.

I do miss intimacy. I have close friends and family members with whom I share intimacy in the form of talk. We tell each other our deepest concerns. But this is still not the boundary-blurring intimacy I'm talking about. It's not the well of clear water you fall into together when you and your lover look into each other's eyes from a few inches away. The last person with whom I had prolonged eye contact was my sister's dog.

At least not having sex simplifies the business of time management. I'm usually doing something else anyway. If I was having sex right now, for example, I wouldn't be writing these sentences, and you wouldn't be reading them. Writing itself provides a kind of connection, although the intimacy between us is one-directional.

And even if I never have sex again, i
to die a virgin, wondering what I missed
included plenty of good times that I won't c
Also, sometimes I had a headache.

libacy is another way to think about not having sex; cy is chosen as a positive path. (Perhaps I could take a active vow of celibacy and get credit for time served.) It's a way to extend your love to the whole universe. If you don't have one particular sexual partner, you are equally married to everyone in the world, even if you've never met them. And not just people, but trees and rocks and streams and stars.

When I swim in Lake Anza in the hills behind Berkeley, I get completely wet. When I lie on my towel on the beach, gravity holds me against the earth and the sun touches whatever part of my body I turn to it. When I take a deep breath, the wind moves into me and fills me up. I'm intimate with water, earth, fire, and air. So, what if I never have sex again? So what?

Still . . .

# Becoming Invisible

When my eighty-three-year-old mother and I took a plane trip together, the wheelchair we had ordered for her was not waiting on the walkway when we got off. The flight attendant said it would be coming shortly, so we stood and stood while all the other deplaning passengers passed us by. Prolonged standing was painful for my mother, and finally she lost it: "Where's my fucking wheelchair? Shit! That's the last time I'll travel on this fucking airline!" I was mortified, but the wheelchair appeared immediately. Once she was seated, she apologized graciously to the flight attendant and they parted on friendly terms.

I, on the other hand, have never had a knack for yelling at people, even when I feel like I'm becoming invisible.

Last week I was waiting to buy envelopes in a crowded stationery store. A vigorous young woman with glistening black hair got waited on first, even though she came in after me, and it wasn't because she pushed her way ahead of me—it was because the cashier didn't notice me.

I, too, even as I become translucent myself, have been guilty of this blindness. Yesterday, standing in line at the post office, I watched a young man at the counter put tape on his packag̶ I was startled when a voice said, "Hi, Sue!" It came from gray-haired woman who was just ahead of me in line—a friend of mine. I'm afraid the reason I hadn't even seen her was that my mind's eye had registered grayness and slid right on by.

I attended a conference of "Buddhist teachers in the West," where two hundred men and women, all mostly older than fifty-five, met together for several days. One distinguished-looking gray-haired man commented to me, "As I look around, I see a lot more gray-haired men than women, and since we're all in about the same age range here, I can only assume that many of the women are dyeing their hair. But these women are Buddhist teachers! Why would a Buddhist teacher dye her hair? You'd think, being a Buddhist, she'd accept herself as she is!" My gray hair was undyed at the time, so he must have assumed self-acceptance on my part.

I tried to tell him: It's not so much that *she* doesn't accept herself as she is but that others don't. It's the invisibility factor. Gray hair shrouds you in fog, and you want to shout, "I'm still here! I still have a physical body! I still have ideas in my head!"

I even have a different understanding of facelifts now. Getting a facelift could be less an act of counterfeiting than an attempt—however futile—to be real, to tear away the veil that society projects onto our faces. I can't blame the sexist, ageist culture for my wrinkles, but it's not the wrinkles themselves that hurt, it's the meaning they are given, a meaning that is mostly unconscious and unspoken.

We see other people get old, but we can't believe we'll succumb. If we remain firm in our resolve, if we exercise and eat the right foods, surely we won't catch the old-age bug. Or science will figure it out for us. A cover of *Harvard Magazine* asked: "Is Aging Necessary?" But thus far, time keeps passing, signing its name across our bodies as it goes.

I'm still on the cusp. I have one foot on each side of the border—the border between getting-old and just-plain-old. It's a shifting border. Remember "Don't trust anyone over thirty"? I recall the time when I thought forty was old, then it was fifty, then it was sixty. But at a certain point, "old" will have no place left to recede to, and, like it or not, I'll be settling my porous bones in a rocking chair on the senior side of the border.

My mother told me she, too, felt invisible as she aged. When she was in her fifties she started an artists' retreat center. She was in her prime; she was taken seriously. But by the time she was seventy, she claimed the board and staff didn't pay any attention to what she said because they thought she was a silly old lady. She sometimes lost her temper and shouted at people in meetings, just as she did on the airplane walkway—she said it was the only way to get people to listen to her. I used to think she was being paranoid, but I'm beginning to see what she means.

In a planning meeting connected with my work, a man brought up a suggestion I had made and credited it to a male colleague about my age: "As Bill so cogently pointed out . . ." I don't believe he was trying to slight me. He must have heard my words when they came out of my mouth, but in his memory, he had heard a man say them. Older men are easier to see than older women. Is it just my imagination, or did my words carry more weight when I was younger and prettier? I don't know. I should also explain that in this case, I was crocheting a shawl during the meeting, so it was partly my fault. If you're a woman over forty-five, it's better not to do any kind of needlework in important meetings.

I'm inspired by the admirable example of the Raging Grannies, who take the stereotype of the little old lady and run with it. They are peace activists who go to demonstrations in theatrical flowered hats and aprons, looking sweet and innocent, which they are not. For example, some Raging Grannies were arrested when they attempted to enlist at a U.S. Army recruiting center in Tucson, saying they wanted to be sent to Iraq so that their grandchildren could come home.

Last year I dyed my gray hair bright red. (There weren't any Buddhist conferences coming up at the time.) My hair was never red all by itself, and I wasn't trying to fool anybody. When the hairdresser asked me what effect I was going for, I said I wanted to do something wild. I said I didn't care if the color didn't look natural, but I *did* want to look . . . well . . . not to put too fine a point on it . . . *younger.* I wanted a hair color that would make people interested in what I had to say.

The hairdresser was expensive but skillful. For about two weeks, the red was very bright, and I was startled to discover that it made a difference. Strangers looked at me directly. From a distance I did look younger, more powerful, maybe even more passionate—a redhead! I became visible to clerks in crowded stores.

After a couple of weeks the color faded to a chemical orange: it's an uphill battle, editing out the marks of age on an aging body. It's expensive, too: if older women didn't mind looking old, a huge sector of the economy would collapse.

I was complaining to my younger sister about feeling invisible as an older woman, like a dry leaf, and I think she felt annoyed with my self-concern, though she didn't say so. She said gently, "What about the idea of dignity? Why don't you cultivate a sense of dignity?" I put the word *dignity* into my pocket like a smooth stone, and held onto it, finding comfort in it.

Not long after, I saw an old woman in the airport in Puerto Vallarta, Mexico. She must have been about ninety. We were both sitting in the departure lounge, waiting for a plane to California. She was wearing turquoise jewelry, a long denim skirt, and a bright pink Mexican shawl, and her extremely wrinkled face, bent over a paperback book, was full of character. Her white hair was rolled into a bun on the back of her head and fastened with wooden sticks—I think they were chopsticks. She looked like an artist, I thought—an *old* artist. She seemed to be traveling alone, but she didn't look afraid or tentative; she looked happy, sitting there reading, with her boarding pass tucked into the pages of her book. She didn't know it, but she was a visitation—a messenger of age. The opposite of invisible, she shone for me— her white hair, her fuchsia shawl. She reminded me not to feel sorry for myself. She got up when they called for early boarding, and walked, slowly and stiffly, with a cane, and smiling, onto the plane. She had dignity.

# The Tomboy Returns

EVENTUALLY I LEARNED how to pass for a woman. I learned to brush my long blonde hair every day, and I wore contact lenses when I was trying to look pretty. From time to time, I even put on a dress without being bribed. I got married, gave birth to two children, nursed them, raised them. But there's a nine-year-old inside of me who still remembers all the good climbing trees in the faraway neighborhood where I grew up, and which shrubs have the straightest twigs to make arrows out of. Surprisingly, the further I get from her in years, the more connected to her I feel. I wish I could make amends to her for the betrayals she suffered.

My children have long since flown, and I've got nobody to make breakfast for. Ever since I passed through menopause, at fifty, and my female organs left me alone again, I have been getting reacquainted with my tomboy self. I honor her adventurous spirit, her brave refusal to be limited by social expectations.

In third grade at school, I was the only girl in Joel's Gang. In order to get in, you had to have a wrestling match with everybody who was already a member. We ran around pretending to be fierce, charging through the middle of the sissy girls' hopscotch games. We practiced wrestling holds on each other and played mumbledy-peg in the forsythia bushes, where the teachers wouldn't see our jackknives.

In those days my mother used to pay me a quarter to put on a dress, on the occasions when a dress was called for—like the visit of a relative. Otherwise I wore dungarees—that's what we called jeans—with a cowboy belt.

With the boys in my neighborhood—Robert and Skipper, Evan and Sammy—I played cops and robbers, and cowboys and Indians: racist, violent games that, years later, I righteously tried to keep my own children from playing. We climbed trees and rode no-hands on our bicycles. I had cap pistols hanging on hooks on my bedroom wall. I traded baseball cards, memorized the batting averages of all the players on the Boston Braves, and played catch by the hour. I read the Hardy Boys mysteries and *Lou Gehrig, Boy of the Sand Lots.* I started the Pirate Club, the Walky-Talky Club, and the Cowboy Comic Collectors Club.

I wore boys' bathing trunks every summer, until I was eight or nine years old. I didn't put on a girls' bathing suit, with all that frilly and deceptive packaging that poked its bones into my flat chest, until another girl taunted me: *You think you're a boy! You think you're a boy!* I was so mad I got out of the swimming pool and hid her clothes in a closet. She had to go home in a wet bathing suit and I pretended I didn't know anything about it.

But why was I in Joel's Gang, instead of playing hopscotch? Perhaps it was my way of refusing to submit.

I think of my parents' body language. My mother didn't seem happy inside her skin. She moved as if trying to hide her body with her body. Other women, too, seemed to move in shuffle and shadow. But in my father's body there was elasticity and readiness. He used to walk a lot, and ride a bicycle. When my mother wanted to go somewhere, she drove a car.

Everywhere I looked, men were running the show, and women were just the helpers: the president and his wife, the school principal and his secretary, the dentist and his hygienist, the pilot and the stewardess. Though I couldn't have stated it consciously, I breathed in the knowledge that a woman's body was not a powerful place to live.

As for me, I wanted to run and jump and climb over fences, even if it meant tearing my clothes. I didn't try to pretend I was a boy, I just wanted to be ungendered, and therefore unlimited. I hated getting my hair cut, for example, and had a wild bush of hair, like a feral child. I didn't want to have to look pretty, but I liked the way I looked in my classy felt cowboy hat—a "real" one like "real" cowboys wore. Far from being a denial of my sexuality, I think my tomboyhood gave me good practice at living in my body and finding pleasure there.

My parents never objected to my bathing trunks or cowboyphilia, and my mother patiently quizzed me on baseball statistics when I asked her to. But I think it wasn't quite OK for me to be a tomboy. I looked up *tomboy* in Doctor Spock, by whose lights I was raised, but he says nothing on the subject. I think my parents must have been at a loss. Perhaps they feared that I would never agree to brush my hair my whole life long and, by logical extension, that I would never become a wife-and-mother.

I think so because in the fourth grade, I was sent to dancing school—ballroom dancing!—years before my schoolmates had to undergo this humiliating rite of passage. I was taught to sit with my ankles crossed until a boy, in parallel agony no doubt, asked me to dance. I learned to do the "box step," an apt name for a spiritless movement that had nothing whatever to do with dancing. ("Step-step-right-together-step-step-left-together.")

For a brief period, I was sent on Sunday afternoons to the home of an elderly Jewish refugee from Vienna who gave me sewing lessons, an activity in which I had no interest whatever. Because I suffered from night terrors and frequent nightmares, I was taken to a child psychiatrist when I was about ten. He asked me intrusive questions like, "Have any of the girls in your class at school begun to menstruate?" It was rumored that one particular girl had already gotten "the curse," but I didn't see that it was any of his business, and so I answered numbly, "I don't know." For Christmas he gave me a perfume-making kit, which I poured down the toilet in disgust.

But there were contradictory messages in my own family. On the one hand, my grandmother told me that I should brush my hair one hundred strokes a day to make it shine. "On doît souffrir pour être belle," she said, with a hint of irony in her voice. One must suffer to be beautiful. On the other hand, a photograph in a family album shows me and my two younger sisters marching around on the lawn at my grandparents' house, pretending to be soldiers, drilling, with sticks over our shoulders for rifles, wearing three-cornered newspaper hats. Grandpa, who came from a military family, was our drill sergeant. We're obviously having a great time, puffing out our childish chests.

I always knew I wasn't a boy. One day I went into the nearby vacant lot that we kids called "the woods." I was carrying my precious handmade bow, and I was looking for arrows. I pushed my way through a tangled arch of bushes, and there was the neighborhood bully, sitting on a stump. He was an archetypal figure, like Butch, the leader of the West Side Gang, in the *Little Lulu* comics I read so avidly. "Give me that bow or pull down your pants," he demanded. Girl that I was, trained to obedience, it never occurred to me that there were any other choices. I handed him the bow.

Not long after, the neighborhood kids gathered in my friend Sammy's back yard for a wrestling tournament. My turn came to wrestle the dreaded bully. I got him to the ground and held him down for the count of ten. I had won! Fair and square. But when I released him and we stood up, I saw that he wanted to kill me for defeating him in public. Terrified, I turned and ran, and he ran after me. I remember the rush of adrenaline that put wings on my heels. I made it safely home, locked the door behind me, and collapsed in fright. The fact that I had just wrestled him to the ground had no transfer value. As soon as the structured contest was over, I went back to being a girl who was scared of a bully.

Another time, Skipper and Evan and I were riding our bicycles around the neighborhood, and we discovered an old carriage house behind a big Victorian house. Upstairs, in the unlocked attic, we searched shamelessly through boxes and found a huge purple jewel, which we stole and buried in Skipper's back yard. We made a treasure map to record the spot—ten paces from the maple tree and fifteen paces from the corner of Skipper's garage—and we solemnly promised each other we'd leave it buried there forever, or at least until we grew up. Then, if one of us was in trouble, we'd dig it up, sell it, and use the money to help that person.

That night I couldn't go to sleep for feeling guilty, and finally I gave in and told my mother about the stolen jewel. The next day, she made us dig it up and take it back and apologize. Luckily, the lady who lived in the Victorian house was not too mad. She explained that the jewel was a glass doorknob. She told us to stay out of her carriage house, and she gave us some cookies. Skipper and Evan were not pleased with me, cookies notwithstanding. Why did I tell? Because I was the only girl? Is that why you shouldn't let women into men's clubs?

Already, by the fifth grade, things had begun to change in ominous ways. Starting that year, girls had to wear skirts or dresses to our school. There was no rule *against* dungarees, however, so I wore both: the dress on top, the blue denim sticking out the bottom. From then on, I had to wear a dress to school. (It's hard to believe now, but when I went to college in the sixties, we weren't allowed to wear pants to class unless it was snowing.)

In sixth grade, the ground continued to shift under my feet. I made friends with girls, some of whom, to my surprise, turned out to have things in common with me. At recess, I sometimes played jacks instead of dodgeball.

By seventh grade, my former playmates in Joel's Gang had lost interest in me. They began dating the very girls whose hopscotch games we had disrupted a few years before—girls who whispered and giggled in the bathroom, girls who wore, to my disgust, tight skirts. Try to climb a tree in a tight skirt!

And then puberty hit, like a curtain coming down. I grew breasts: tender objects which weren't there before, bodies on top of my body. They came like strangers, and I was supposed to welcome them as part of myself, even though I'd lived all twelve years of my life without them. The left one started first, and I remember examining myself in the mirror and worrying that the right one would never catch up.

Then, when I was thirteen, I woke up one morning with dried blood on my pajama bottoms. I didn't know what it was at first, because I had imagined that the "the curse" would come in a red flood that would run out from under my desk and along the classroom floor. My mother gave me a pad, and explained how to attach it. Perhaps no one is still menstruating who remembers those horrible elastic belts with hooks in front and back. She was pleased and supportive; but I felt ashamed—I had been claimed by my tribe, marked irrevocably as a second-class citizen. I would be one of them after all. My tree-climbing days were over.

I certainly couldn't buck biology, and it didn't occur to me until much later that I could buck the social definitions that went with it. And so I began to behave accordingly. I tried to please my teachers, to look pretty, to act polite. I grew my hair, and brushed it. At school dances I waited in silent terror that I wouldn't be asked to dance. If asked, I danced in an agony of shyness, unable to think of anything to say. In high school, by a strange twist of fate, I was invited to a formal prep school dance by Joel, of Joel's Gang. We had barely spoken to each other since the third grade. We fox-trotted together, speechless and miserable, no longer able to practice wrestling holds on each other.

All during college and into my twenties, I spurned athletic pursuits as being somehow for stupid people, especially if those people were female. Enthusiasm for physical activity had come to mean the opposite of smart, hip, and sexy. Physical exuberance was gone. I wore constricting undergarments. I hoped I wouldn't sweat, and that the wind wouldn't muss my hair. I now see *this* as my betrayal of my sex—this nice resignation, this alienation from the body called "femininity."

Now I go to a gym and I lift weights. I want muscles—muscles that show. I like the way they look. I like to feel strong. I like to do the bench press, to shove that big heavy bar up off my chest. If I was wrestling with the bully, I probably couldn't push him off me, but I'd sure try.

As I get older I'm coming back around to where I was before puberty. I may not wear a boy's bathing suit again, but I'm urging myself to ignore what's considered appropriate. My body is no longer limber enough to climb trees, but it's a good time to cultivate a limber and unladylike mind.

I spent a huge chunk of my life trying to look attractive and more or less succeeding. The habit dies hard. Given a choice, I'd rather be pretty than ugly, but at this point the whole matter of physical beauty is becoming irrelevant—just as it was when I was nine—and in this there is some measure of relief.

For years, one of my noticeable features was a great mass of thick blonde hair. Then the time came when I wanted, as Yeats said, to be "loved for myself alone and not my yellow hair." I cut my hair short, and now I own neither hairbrush nor comb. This cutting off has been both liberating and terrifying.

It's not just a question of how I look. There's the more important matter of behavior. When I was a tomboy, I organized cudgel tournaments. Now my creative projects are less athletic than when I was nine, but I try to rediscover that brave spirit, that determination to follow my heart. When I was nine I didn't waste my time being nice. I didn't do other people's laundry, or read the manuscripts of people I'd never met, for free, just as a favor. My nine-year-old self thinks it might be fun to learn to play the drums, or go on retreat to a Benedictine monastery in northern California, where I can stay in a cottage made of a wine barrel and read about saints.

I'm grateful for my tomboy time, because, as my grandmother used to say, "old age is not for sissies." If I hadn't had all that practice climbing forbidden trees, I might slip more easily into loneliness and fear as I grow old.

The crone who's knocking at my front door is not a stranger— she's the girl in dungarees, her hair a glad tangle, come to guide me back to my bravest self. She says I never have to brush my hair again, unless I want to.

# PART THREE

# In the Realm of the Spirit

# Tea with God

As a child, I worried about whether or not to believe in God. He was hardly ever mentioned in our family, except in my mother's exclamations, so I didn't know if he was real or not, but if he was and I didn't believe in him, I thought it would hurt his feelings. I decided to try and make contact, by making a place for him where he knew he'd be welcome. It was under a forsythia bush in our back yard, in the cave formed by its hanging branches. Inside that dim chapel, I cleared the ground of leaves and, though I didn't know what an altar was, I built a fairy table out of twigs and mud, about six inches high. I covered it with a tablecloth I made out of the heads of pansies, blue and purple, laid like overlapping shingles. I sat there in the close-to-dark, pleased with the holy place of mud I'd made. I wanted to talk to God, but I didn't know what to say, so I just sat there.

The next day I crawled back in and saw that the place I had fixed up for God was now alive with big black ants. They drove like tiny cars in a traffic jam across the top of the altar, dragging away with them large pieces of the pansy petals for their larder. They had wrecked it—it was gross, not holy at all. I didn't think God would ever come to this place even if he did exist.

When I was a teenager, I went to Quaker meeting and tried to talk to God there, but I only worried about my French homework. What was wrong with me? I found that if I closed my eyes and rolled them up inside my head, and aimed them at the place above my nose where Hindus put a red spot, I felt something new and strange—a vertigo, a lifting, verging on a headache. Could this be God? If so, he didn't speak to me, nor I to him, and after a while I gave up that method.

When my son Sandy was four, he said, "I just found out how you can see God." He was lying down in the back seat of the car (in the days before car seats), on the way home from nursery school. "You squeeze your eyes shut, as tight as you can, and you see a blue light, and that's God."

I tried it myself—later, of course, not while I was driving— but it didn't work for me.

When I began to practice Zen, it didn't matter any more whether I could talk to God or he to me—Zen people don't go in for that. It was a relief to stop worrying about God for a while, though now I worried that I didn't know how to meditate. It looked like I was meditating from the outside, but I was just sitting there, thinking random thoughts, and breathing. Nothing was happening. That's what I still do—just sit, and nothing still happens. By now I've gotten used to it. I've learned that that's what Zen practice is: "just sitting." Still, sometimes it feels lonesome.

I have no mate; I sleep alone. When I rise, I always drink a cup of green tea, and I watch the day begin. I brew the tea for four minutes in a red iron pot with dragonflies on it, and then I pour it into a white cup with a blue rim.

On Sundays I don't set the alarm. One Sunday not so long

ago I opened my eyes to a foggy morning. The bed was warm, and I didn't have any place I had to go. I thought with pleasure about how good it was going to be to drink my tea. But the catch was, I didn't want to get out of bed.

I had no idea I was going to speak, but suddenly, to my surprise, I said out loud, "God, I have a favor to ask you. Would you bring me a cup of green tea?" It seemed a small thing to ask, especially when you consider that I had never really asked God for anything before.

Then God answered me, out loud, and that surprised me, too. His voice came out of my own mouth.

"I'm sorry, Sue," he said. "I would if I could, but I don't have the arms and legs the job calls for. But I completely support you in getting yourself a cup of tea. I'm with you all the way!"

I saw that he really wasn't going to do it. "But God," I said, "I don't have *anybody* to bring me tea in bed."

God said, "That's not my fault. The fact that there's nobody in the bed with you is the result of choices you yourself have made. Anyway, I'm right here. I'll be glad to go down to the kitchen with you."

I could tell that he meant it, and I was deeply touched. I tossed back the quilt with a burst of zeal, and swung my bare feet to the cold floor.

I heard God say, just under his breath this time, "You go, Sue!"

While the tea brewed, I had four minutes to think of the times when I *had* had a man in the morning bed, and as far as I could remember, no one had ever brought me tea on Sunday morning. Maybe I never asked.

I sat on the porch with the blue-rimmed cup in my hands. The tea slaked my thirst, and I just sat there, watching a squirrel who was eating the buds of the passionflower vine on the roof next door.

# I Wasn't My Self

I WANT TO TELL YOU about coming apart, wanting to die, and returning at last to myself, and about how my Buddhist practice both helped and hindered me in this zigzag journey.

Although I was suffering from severe depression, I didn't call it that for most of the several years I was in and out of it. I thought depression was for lethargic people who lay around in bed all day. But my pain was as sharp as an ice pick. Restless in the extreme, I paced and paced, looking for a way out. The visible cause was the drawn-out and difficult end of a relationship. The invisible causes were old griefs and fears, and other conditions unknown to me. In my fifties, I fell down a rabbit hole in time, away from grown-uphood, into the helplessness of a two-year-old.

It's taboo to be depressed. When I was feeling really bad, I still went to work, though I was barely functional. If I had had the flu and had been in a fraction of the pain I was in, I would have called in sick. But I didn't call in "depressed." One day I threw into the computer's trash can a whole issue of the magazine I was editing, thinking I was saving it. Then I emptied the trash. I had to hire a consultant to look for it in the virtual garbage, and eventually I got most of it back. But it was myself I wanted to put in the trash.

———

Physical pain is hard to describe, and psychic pain is even harder. I was in intense, moment-by-moment pain, and all I wanted was to get away from it. The pain was in the thoughts, which I didn't, and couldn't, recognize as just my thoughts. (As Buddha said, "When, for you, in the thought is just the thought, then you shall be free . . .") A voice in my head repeated what I took to be The Truth: that I was completely alone, that I would never again love or be loved by another person, that "I" was nothing.

I spent hours every day on the phone. Once, during the forty-five-minute drive from my boyfriend's home back to Berkeley, I had to stop and call a friend from a pay phone by the side of the road, so that I could drive the rest of the way home, even though it was only another fifteen minutes away. Luckily she was home. "I just got off the Richmond Bridge," I sobbed. "I'm afraid I don't exist. My body's here, but there's nobody in it."

"You exist," she said. "How could I love you if you didn't exist? Come over right now and we'll take a walk on the Berkeley pier."

I've gained some understanding of what it must be like to have an invisible illness, like lupus, or chronic fatigue syndrome. I wished I could wear a sign around my neck—"I might look OK, but I'm sick!"—so people wouldn't expect me to be functional.

I couldn't eat—a common symptom of depression. It wasn't just loss of appetite. Chewing itself was unbearable. A blob of bread was scary because it got in the way of breathing, and breathing was already hard enough to do. Liquids were more manageable. It occurs to me now that I'd regressed to the stage before I had teeth, when the only kind of eating I could do was sucking. So now I drank hot milk with honey, and Earl Grey tea. I lost a lot of weight, something I'm always trying to do when I feel "normal," but I was too downhearted to take any pleasure from it.

Like many other depressed people, I didn't sleep well. I clutched my pillow and called out to the flapping curtains for help. I took sleeping pills—sometimes they worked, sometimes they didn't. I couldn't read my way through the sleepless patches of the night (or during the day, either, for that matter) because I couldn't get past the fear to concentrate on anything.

Waking in the morning was the worst of all. The moment consciousness returned, the pain came with it. *Oh no! I have to breathe my way through another day.*

I didn't like getting into the shower because I didn't want to be alone with my skin. To feel my own skin and imagine that nobody would ever touch it again was unbearable. Better to swaddle myself in layers, no matter what the weather, so the skin didn't have to notice it was alone. I remembered a pale young woman who had lived next door to me years before, who began to wear more and more layers of clothing—a skirt over her pants, a dress over her skirt, a long shirt over her dress, then a sweater, a long coat, a cape, a hat—in Berkeley summer weather. Finally her father came and took her away to a mental hospital.

One of the worst things about being so depressed is that one becomes totally self-absorbed. I could hear other people only when they were talking to me about *me:* recommending homeopathic remedies, interpreting my dreams to me, telling me they loved me.

During my depression, one of my adult sons had a serious bicycle accident, and my fear for his well-being snapped me out of my self-absorption for the five days that he was in the hospital. I sat all night in a chair beside his hospital bed, hypervigilant, watching him sleep. I put a cool cloth on his forehead. I prayed to whomever was listening, making a promise I couldn't keep: not to be depressed if only he would be all right.

He came home to my house from the hospital, with one leg in a full cast, because he needed to be taken care of for a little while. It was summer—he sat on the back porch of the house he'd grown up in, in the sun, and I washed his back.

One day I walked into the living room where he was reading on the couch, and he said, "My God, what's the matter? You look like a ghost!"

Dry-mouthed with panic, I told him I had to go see my boyfriend; we had to decide *right then* whether to break up. "Do you think I should stay with him?" I asked.

My son looked at me with an expression I'll never forget—a mixture of despair and love. "I don't know how to help you any more," he said. "I don't think you should be driving, in the state you're in. Can't you stay here and be my mother?"

But I couldn't. I drove out to see the man, compelled by an irrational sense of urgency, with my son's stricken face burning in my mind.

I had been a Zen Buddhist practitioner for many years, and I assumed that my meditation practice would steady me. What could be more comforting than forty minutes in the peaceful, familiar zendo, with the sweet smell of tatami straw matting? But it didn't help. This is what I want to say: at times it made things worse. The demons in my mind took advantage of the silence. They weren't real demons, but they didn't care whether they were real or not; they tormented me anyway.

My Buddhist teachers encouraged me to keep on sitting zazen. "Just watch the painful thoughts arise," they said, "and watch them pass away again."

When I sat down on a zafu, the painful thoughts arose all right, but if they passed away, it was only to make room for even more painful thoughts. *I'll die alone.* And, adding insult to injury: *I'm the worst Zen student that ever was.*

When I told one of my teachers I was disappointed that zazen didn't make me feel better, she said, "You don't sit zazen to *get* something. You sit zazen in order to sit zazen. If you want zazen to make you feel better, it won't work." But didn't Buddha invent Buddhism in the first place to alleviate suffering? Did all those other people in the zendo *really* get up out of bed at five in the morning for no particular reason?

Still, I kept going back, hoping that if I meditated hard enough I'd have some sort of "breakthrough." In the past, sitting in the zendo, I, too, had had the experience of watching my worries turn to dry powder and blow away. So I signed up to sit *rohatsu sesshin*, the weeklong intensive meditation retreat in early December that commemorates Buddha's enlightenment. He sat down under the bodhi tree and vowed not to get up until he saw the truth. It took him a week. I had sat many sesshins before, but maybe this would be my week.

The first day was bad. I cried quietly, not wanting to disturb the others. The second day was worse. Tears and snot dripped off my chin onto my breast. I hated myself. *Nobody else will ever love me!*

"Bring your attention back to your breathing," my teachers had advised me. This was like telling a person on the rack, whose arms are being pulled out of her shoulder sockets, to count her exhalations.

And yet I wasn't on the rack. I was in the familiar zendo. Around me sat my dharma brothers and sisters, hands in their pretty mudras. As for *my* mudra, I dug the nails of my left hand deep into the palm of my right hand, feeling relief at the simple physical pain, and momentary proof of my existence.

On the third day, during a break, I snuck away to a pay phone down the street and called my sister in Philadelphia. Choking on my own words, I told her I didn't know who I was. I wasn't exactly convinced by her reassurances, but just hearing her voice was some comfort.

The fourth day was worse yet. The distance between me and the people on either side of me was infinite, even though their half-lotus knees were only six inches away from mine. I thought of the man who wasn't going to be taking care of me after all.

*I'm nobody*, I thought. *There's nobody here at all*. This feeling of no-self was supposedly the point of meditation, and yet I had somehow gotten onto the wrong path. While a nameless pressure mounted inside me, the people around me just kept sitting zazen. I couldn't stay another second—I left without getting permission from the sesshin director.

Driving away from the zendo in the privacy of my car, I shouted: "This is the worst day of my life!" (There would be other days after that when I would say it again: "No, *this* day is worse.")

I drove into Tilden Park and walked into the woods, where no one could see me. I screamed and pulled my hair. I lay down on the ground and rolled down the hill, letting the underbrush scratch and poke me. I liked having leaves get stuck in my hair and clothing. It made me feel real. I picked up a fallen branch from a redwood tree and began flailing myself on the back. The bodily pain was easier to bear than the mental pain it pushed aside.

But I scared myself. How could I be spending my sesshin afternoon beating myself with sticks in the woods? How had it come to this?

I picked the leaves out of my hair and went home. The next morning, the fifth day, I called the Zen center and said I wasn't feeling well—an understatement if there ever was one—and wouldn't be sitting the rest of the sesshin. I didn't sit zazen for some months after that.

I thought I had failed in my practice—decades of it!—and was bitterly disappointed in myself. Only later, after the depression subsided, did I see what a growth it was. Choosing not to sit was choosing not to be ruled by dogma, to be compassionate with myself, to take my spiritual practice into my own hands.

Buddhism teaches that we have "no fixed self." There is nothing permanent about me. During the depression, I wasn't my "self," as we say. I didn't seem to have a self at all, in a way that cruelly mimicked this central point in Buddhist teaching. You'd think that it would be painless to have no self, because without a self, who was there to be in pain? And yet it was unbearable. Like a wind-up doll, I went stiffly through the motions of being Sue Moon, but there was no person present, no aliveness—only a battery that was running down.

I felt angry at Buddhism: *You told me there's no fixed self, and I believed you, and look where it got me!* I knew the yang of it but not the yin—the balancing truth that there was no separation.

I couldn't have gone on like this indefinitely; I was tearing up the fabric of my life. As I was weeping to a friend on the phone one afternoon, speaking my familiar litany, she suddenly shouted at me: "Stop it! You've got to save your own life! You've got to do it! Nobody else but you can save yourself, and you *can* do it! You just have to be brave. That's all there is to it." This was an important phone call: she startled me into finding a stick of courage, and I held onto it by reminding myself of her words.

Still, the misery continued, and I finally decided to try medication. I had a lot of resistance to overcome. I thought my unhappiness had two parts: negative circumstances in the outside world, which an antidepressant obviously couldn't fix, and negative attitudes inside my head, which I thought my Buddhist practice should take care of. And after all, the monks of old had managed without SSRIs.

But I had to do something different to save my own life, as my friend had said, and medication was something I hadn't tried. I consulted a psychiatrist, who prescribed a common antidepressant. I took it for about a week and felt much worse, though I wouldn't have thought it possible to feel worse a week before. The psychiatrist had me stop that brand and try another. I felt it kick in after a couple of days. I didn't feel drugged; rather, as though a deadly fog was lifting.

The antidepressant I was taking was supposed to be good for

people who have trouble with obsessional thinking, and I seem to be one of those. The medication did what zazen didn't do—it quieted the voices in my head: "I'm lost. I'm nothing." It didn't shut them up entirely, but they were no longer screaming, and I was sometimes able to tune them out.

As to the monks of old, I now wonder if some of them obsessed their lives away in misery and if others left the monastery because they couldn't concentrate. Buddhist history doesn't tell us about the ones who tried and failed, the ones with attention deficit disorder or clinical depression.

One day, offhandedly, I signed up for a beginning photography class, without thinking much about it. Perhaps a deeper intuition told me that this would be another door out of my misery. I'm a writer, but words failed me in the worst times. Taking pictures required me to look outside myself. It didn't matter whether I had a self or not, the light kept right on shining, laying itself out on surfaces, like a Tibetan monk doing full prostrations. The world gave itself to me, wordlessly, through my camera. I remember my elation as my first print swam into the red glow of the darkroom at the community art center: my nieces, one big, one little, standing in the kitchen doorway in the sun, in overalls, grinning. I didn't have to understand myself. I didn't have to make anything. My camera led me to what was already beautiful. Learning a new skill made me feel alive.

I was also learning to trust myself. Taking an antidepressant and stopping sitting were acts of faith in myself. So, too, I learned to construct my own spiritual practice.

Every morning, as soon as I got out of bed, I lit a candle on my little altar, and offered a stick of incense. I made three full bows, then stood before the altar, my palms pressed together, and recited out loud my morning prayers, starting with a child's prayer a Catholic friend had taught me:

Angel of God, my guardian dear,
To whom God's love commits me here,
Ever this day be at my side
To watch and guard, to rule and guide.

It was comforting to ask somebody else, somebody who wasn't me, to help me. Prayer was something I missed in Zen practice as I knew it, so I imported it from Christianity, and other Buddhist traditions. I prayed to Tara, the Tibetan goddess of compassion, to fly down from the sky, all green and shining, into my heart. I prayed to Prajna Paramita, the mother of all Buddhas, who, as the Prajna Paramita Sutra tells us, "brings light so that all fear and distress may be forsaken, and disperses the gloom and darkness of delusion."

Then I took refuge in Buddha, dharma, and sangha, saying the words out loud, whether I felt anything or not.

That I had shaped this practice for myself gave me confidence. And the early morning incense smoke, though it was thin and drifting, provided a hint of continuity for my days. They seemed, after all, to be days in the same life. One person's life—mine.

Now I can say this: there are times in life when nothing helps, when you just have to feel terrible for a while. All you can do is go through the agony and come out the other end of it. It's a gift, in a way, to hit the bottom, though it didn't feel like a gift at the time. If you lie on the grass, you can't fall down.

There's a saying in Zen that "inquiry and response come up together." Perhaps that's what prayer is. To make an inquiry is already to get a response, because asking implies that there's something else there. And there's not even a time lag. The moment you're asking for help, you're already getting it, though it may not be the help you thought you wanted.

Once, when I called Zen teacher Reb Anderson in despair, he came to Berkeley to see me. We sat on a park bench in a children's playground, and he told me, "The universe is already ✓ taking care of you." I said this mantra to myself over and over: "The universe is already taking care of me."

A turning moment came at the end of a hard summer while I was visiting friends on Cape Cod. One late afternoon I walked barefoot and alone down the beach and into the salty water. There were no people about, so I took off my bathing suit in the water and flung it up on the sand. I swam and swam and felt the water touching every part of me. I was *in* it—no dry place left. I wasn't afraid to be alone with my skin because I wasn't alone; there was nothing, not the width of a cell, between me and the rest of the universe. I did a somersault under the water and looked up at the shiny membrane above me. My head hatched into the light, and I breathed the air and knew that I would be all right. No, not *would be,* but *was already.* I was back in my life.

Now, many years out of the desolation, I still don't know why I suffered so much, or why I stopped. I can neither blame myself for the suffering nor take credit for its cessation.

I sit again—I mean in meditation—but not as much as I used to. I also bow and chant and pray. I stopped taking the antidepressant, though I'd return to it without shame if I thought it would be useful.

I practice curiosity. Curiosity doesn't sound like a very spiritual quality, but I mean it so. What is it to be born a human being? What does it mean to be embodied in your separate skin? There are many paths out of the delusion of separation besides having a boyfriend—things like writing and swimming, for example. And there's studying this human life. You could call it Buddhadharma, or you could call it something else—it doesn't matter.

I'm now willing to admit that I sit zazen for a reason: I want to understand who, if anybody, I am and how I'm connected to the rest of it. And yes, I want to stop suffering and I want to help others stop suffering.

I've gained some confidence from surviving those terrible years, and the older I get the easier it becomes to follow the good advice of the bumper sticker: "Don't believe everything you think." There's steadiness in age.

# You Can't Take It with You

AND WHAT YOU LEAVE behind should be sorted into boxes and neatly labeled.

The old house I've lived in for over thirty-five years has an attic, right under the roof. I can stand up easily under the peak, but the roof slopes down on the sides and I have to be careful not to puncture my scalp on the sharp ends of the shingle nails that come right through from the other side, as I'm foraging for a pair of mittens in a box of snow clothes.

To get to the mittens I might have to push aside boxes of books and papers, my grown sons' childhood collections of bottle caps and souvenir spoons, the pinhole camera I made in a weekend workshop, a box of vinyl record albums, or my rusty bookbinding tools. When I'm downstairs in the relatively uncluttered living room, I can feel these possessions pressing on me from the other side of the ceiling. They are heavy and growing heavier; I fear they are making baby boxes at night when I'm not looking.

Every few years I make a stab at it. This time I've hired my niece to help me. We pull the boxes one by one from the shadows, and we sit on milk crates and examine the contents. Some of the boxes are chewed at the corners and one has a nest made of a shredded high school yearbook. The rats were persuaded to depart years ago by an exterminator, at no small expense to me, but we find a few unsprung traps, still baited with dried-up peanut butter, in the corners of the eaves.

From a box full of unsorted letters I pull one out at random; it's from a homesick child at camp. I lose my bearings, the past tugs at me. Do I owe it to my children to keep these things? Do I owe it to my children to throw them away? Feeling weak and demoralized, I label the box: LETTERS TO SORT, and my niece pushes it back under the eaves and pulls out the next one.

When I was a child, I played in my grandmother's attic, dressing up from the costume trunk and playing with the old doll's house. When my grandmother was a child, she played in that very same attic—it was *her* grandmother's attic. After my mother died, my siblings and I had to deal with the contents of the attic—boxes of letters that went back five generations and a trunk of antique dresses. We gave the letters to a historical library, and the dresses we brought to a family reunion, where we had a fashion show. We older ones watched while the young women of the family—nieces, daughter-in-law, nephew's girlfriend—walked out one at a time onto our makeshift runway in the middle of the living room and modeled the dresses: Cousin Lizzie Wentworth's taffeta traveling dress, Grandma's flapper dress, Aunt Bessie's purple lace ball gown. They sashayed, they paused, they held up their trains, they lifted their chins coquettishly, and they brought the old dresses to life. When they returned to their various homes they took with them the dresses they wanted.

I watch the various ways my contemporaries cope with objects as they get older. One friend, each year at her birthday party, requires of her guests that they choose one of her books to take home. A negative example is provided by the friend who can't stop acquiring things. He loves tools of every kind, and whenever he drives past a broken toaster oven, he stops to put it in his trunk. "But you already have a broken toaster oven!" I exclaim.

"I can fix it. Someone might need one." His friends now give him their broken bicycles and old lamps, saving themselves the trouble of carting them to the dump. There's only a narrow path through his living room, between piles of things he's scavenged from the curbside trash. Sometimes, it's true, he fixes an old weedcutter and gives it away, but he himself admits that the situation has become unmanageable and he's almost given up trying to gain control.

My sister sold her house in Berkeley a year ago. She put all her possessions in storage except for what she could fit into her car, and she drove with her dog to New Mexico and rented a tiny house in the desert. She likes the simplicity of her life there. She has pointed out to me that I could put my belongings in storage, too, if I want a simpler life. I wouldn't even have to go to the trouble of moving—I could just stay on in my nice bare house. But there's the cost of storage to consider.

I have posted a sign on the wall over my desk: "Don't think for a minute you're not going to die." Believe it or not, this sign makes me happy every time I notice it. It invigorates me, like a slap on the back from an old friend, reminding me that I'm not dead yet.

A couple of years ago, I joined a group called a "Year-to-Live" group. Ten of us and our skillful leader met once a month for a year, pretending we only had a year to live, in order to practice being fully alive, not sweating the small stuff, letting go of extras.

One of our last assignments, to help us practice letting go, was to give away something that was precious to us. After all, we'll have to give away every last thing in the end. We each drew our secret Santa name out of a hat. I liked Michael, the young man whose name I drew, and I walked around my house with him in mind, looking at the special objects on shelves and windowsills, and I finally settled on a Japanese tea bowl. My grandmother had gotten it long ago in Japan, and it always sat with pride of place on the mantelpiece in her living room. When she died, I asked for that cup. My mother was at first reluctant, feeling the cup should stay in its spot on the mantel, but my sister persuaded her, saying, "Give it to her! She's a Zen Buddhist—she needs a Japanese tea bowl."

Before I wrapped the tea bowl up for Michael, I felt the cool round clay in my hands and admired the mottled brown glaze one last time. It was a stretch to let go of it, but that was the point, wasn't it? Generosity surged in my breast; I was proud of myself.

At our final meeting, we went around the circle opening our gifts, and each giver told the story of the object. Michael loved the bowl—he said he looked forward to drinking tea out of it. I was the last person to open my gift, and it turned out that Michael, by coincidence, had drawn my name. My gift from him was a smooth stone about two inches wide with the word *gratitude* and a daisy painted on it. While Michael told the story of how he had bought the stone one special weekend when he and his girlfriend were on a yoga retreat in the desert, how that was the very day they decided to marry, how he always kept it on his altar, I was thinking, "*Gratitude* indeed! So this is what I get in exchange for an ancient Japanese tea bowl!"

Deeply shocked by this upwelling of mean-spiritedness, I placed the gratitude stone on my own altar at home, thinking to keep it there as a training device until I could look at it and actually feel gratitude. I reminded myself that the stone was probably just as precious to Michael as the tea bowl was to me. But it wasn't working—the more I looked at it the less grateful I felt, and it was a relief, finally, to give it to the Goodwill store along with some old sweaters. I'm OK about the tea bowl though.

The Zen poet Ryokan lived in a simple hut in the mountains of Japan. The story goes that a thief came to his hut one evening and found nothing to steal. Ryokan came home and caught him. "You have come a long way," he said to the thief, "and you shouldn't leave empty-handed. Please take my clothes as a gift."

The bewildered thief took the clothes and slunk away. Ryokan sat naked, watching the moon, and wrote the following poem:

> The thief left it behind:
> the moon
> at my window

When he was an old man, Ryokan and a young nun named Teishin fell in love, and they exchanged letters and poems. In Ryokan's very last years she moved to a hut nearby and took care of him. After Ryokan's death, their correspondence was published along with his collected poems. Luckily for us, Ryokan must have kept all Teishin's letters in a shoebox in the corner of his hut.

My niece and I have looked inside all of the boxes in the attic. Some we got rid of entirely. Some we condensed. All are labeled, even if only with the words PAPERS TO SORT. I may have another crack at them one of these days, but in the meantime, I'm letting go of letting go. And inside each box of papers I've put a note that says, "Feel free to throw this away."

# The Secret Place

When I was a child, I found a secret place in the bayberry bushes. It was summer, when my family floated free from the known world, the world that was measured by carpools and sidewalks, and went to the seashore. I was lonely there, alone in my separate self, in my dungaree shorts, with dirty knees and poison ivy between my toes.

I would put my jackknife in my pocket and wind my way through a scratchy gap in the bushes into a clearing the size of a small room, an almost flat place on the flank of a hill, overlooking Menemsha Pond. The bayberry bushes were taller than I was, and my parents couldn't see me from the house. They didn't even know the secret place existed. But I could see far across the water to the shimmering dunes of Lobsterville.

In this bushy room I practiced cartwheels and handstands, turning the world upside down. I sat on the grass and whittled sticks. I could see time passing by watching the sails move across the pond.

Back in the house, my father was depressed, shut up in his study writing something all the time. My mother tied her hair up in a bandanna and tried to keep us kids from bothering him. My little sisters chased each other around the house, screeching. I felt the tension of our family life, a sadness I couldn't cure, couldn't even name as sadness.

I lay on my back on the ground that was crunchy with lichen, while the sky did cartwheels around me. As the day came to an end, the sun's light turned a thicker and thicker yellow, and clouds rushed away from me into the void on the other side of the horizon and disappeared. This daily ending, staged with the smell of the bayberry and the crying of the gulls, gave me a lump in my throat—a shout I couldn't shout out.

I had no playmates my own age and we had no near neighbors—my schoolteacher father liked to get away from people in the summer. My sisters were considerably younger than I was, and they were occupied with each other. But it wasn't just someone to play with that I wanted—it was being part of something bigger than me.

I read Howard Pyle's *Robin Hood* and made plans to start a Robin Hood club when we got back to town in the fall. My friends and I would learn to fight with cudgels, and we'd defend the little kids in the neighborhood against the bullies. I would be Little John, who was big and kind, my favorite of Robin Hood's band. I found a big stick of driftwood on the beach and practiced air-fighting with my cudgel—I made it sing as I swung it through the air.

Books from the public library were company. One summer I went through all of Louisa May Alcott's novels, in their plain cloth library bindings stamped in gold on the spine. I went kite flying with Jo and her boys in *Jo's Boys*, and then with my own family in what's called real time, on a day when my father wasn't so depressed. He was the captain of the kite, a big green one we called the Green Dragon; he was a sailor, and this was another kind of sail. We got the kite aloft, and it grew smaller and smaller as it rose closer to the half moon. Then my father held onto the spool of string and we walked down the hill, climbed into the rowboat, and pushed off from the beach. My father let me put on garden gloves and hold the string while the kite pulled us, frictionless, across the pond. It was magic, as if God himself was up there in the air pulling us along, though my parents didn't speak of God.

I wondered about God. I wondered who I was and what I was doing there. Why was there only my one small self inside my head, serving a life sentence in the solitary confinement of my skull, looking out of my eye sockets? It didn't make sense.

The summer I was ten I had insomnia, although I didn't know that word, and I was afraid I was going to die for lack of sleep. I lay in my bed listening for the ship's clock as it chimed the watches of the night. Eight bells for midnight. The worst thing about the loneliness was that it was unspeakable. I couldn't describe it or explain it. Nothing was wrong, but I was lost. Two bells meant one in the morning. I tiptoed into my parents' room. "I can't go to sleep," I said.

I wanted to get into bed with my parents, but I didn't dare ask. I was too old. My mother told me to imagine sheep jumping over a fence and to count them. It seemed like a dumb idea that had nothing to do with the fear that kept me awake, but I was willing to give it a try. "If you get up to a hundred sheep and you're still awake, come back," she said.

I did—I got to a hundred, easy. "Could a person die from not sleeping?" I asked my mother. "No," she said, "No one ever died from not sleeping. Why don't you read your book, sweetie?"

Back in my bed I read *Under the Lilacs*, about an orphan boy and his dog, and how they ran away from the circus. Four bells for two in the morning—I saw the curtains shifting like breath in the moonlight. Six bells for three in the morning, as the moonlight faded and pulsed again in a silent, scary whoosh— caused unbeknownst to me by a passing cloud—and then I must have slept, because I never heard the end of the night watch.

In the morning I walked barefoot to the secret place, watching out for poison ivy. I wanted the soles of my feet to be as tough as an Indian's by the end of the summer. There had been a light mist in the night, and so the pale green lichen was wet and soft.

I imagined myself an orphan in the wilderness. I would have to gather berries and build a shelter for myself in order to survive. I made a little one first, for practice. I snapped off some twigs from the bayberry bushes and whittled away the little bumps. When I had a nice pile of smooth twigs no more than six inches long, I constructed a lean-to with them, using long grass to join the twigs at the joints. I put some stones and shells from the beach inside it, to serve as chairs and tables for the fairies. I didn't exactly believe in fairies, but I assumed there were unseen forces in the universe and I wanted to contact them. They were either very small or very large.

When I lay on my stomach and stuck my face into the sweet-smelling grass, I saw a little red dot that revealed itself to be a spider when it crawled up a blade of grass. To that spider I was as big as a whole world. Then I rolled over on my back, being careful not to crush the spider, and looked at the clouds—the layers of them, some so far up that they made the near clouds seem to move in the opposite direction. Compared to them I was a little red spider. I was microscopic and huge at the same time.

I practiced handstands, and the more I practiced the longer I could stay up. I liked the part where I kicked up the second foot, when the momentum took over and inverted the world. In those days I didn't need a wall to practice against, as I do now in my yoga class. I wanted to be able to walk on my hands. I could take the first step—could pick up my right hand and quickly put it down again a few inches forward before I fell—but I wanted to take a second step with the left hand. Patiently, I practiced. It seemed important. When my shoulders got tired, I sat on the grass to rest and rearranged the fairies' furniture in their lean-to. "OK, fairies," I said. "Watch me walk on my hands." I swung my feet up against the sky and this time I took two steps with my hands before I came down. I gave a whoop. Robin Hood would be proud of me. Maybe I'd even join the circus.

My parents didn't worry that I was wandering around exploring the natural world by myself; they knew I would follow their only rule: not to go swimming alone. The only other local hazard was poison ivy. They didn't know I was full of longing for something I couldn't name, because I didn't tell them.

"Susie! Time for lunch!" came my mother's voice. The other world was calling, the middle-sized world.

As I get older, I find myself coming back to childhood's yearning. I both seek solitude and fear it, just as I did at ten. Upstairs in my study in the quiet house, I'm drinking my green tea and sitting sideways in my favorite chair, with my feet hanging over one arm like a teenager, looking out the window at the redwood tree. I'm wondering who I am and what I'm doing here in this bag of skin, as the old Chinese Zen masters called it. Why am I *still* the only one inside?

Twice, I wasn't alone in my body. I could feel the company inside as I watched the bulge of a foot move across my belly. I liked having someone else with me, for a change, in the small apartment of my body, though of course I liked it even more when each of the babies came out to meet me.

If I had a partner I expect it would take the sharp edge off the longing, but I'm talking about something other than being single here, a more essential separation; I'm not talking about being alone in my bed—that's another conversation—but about being alone in my head.

I sit in meditation at home and I go out to sit with others in Buddhist practice places. Sometimes I sit in the teacher's seat, sometimes I sit in the seat of a student, and always I sit in longing. In that slow turn between the outbreath and the inbreath, the question sometimes arises: "How do I get out of this separate self?"

In the Zen tradition we usually face the wall and so can't see each other. When I sat recently with people from the Theravadan tradition, we sat in a circle facing each other with our eyes closed. I snuck a peek at the others, all of them seeming to sit so peacefully, and I thought, "What are they all doing and how do they know how to do it?" A wave of longing vibrated in my blood like a shot of brandy, and I felt hot prickles all over my skin. I said to myself, "Hello, longing. I know you." And in that moment I suddenly felt happy. I liked the prickles. And for the hundred thousandth time, I returned to my breathing, letting the air in the room come into my lungs like the tide—the same air that was flowing in and out of all the other bodies in the room, joining us together. Longing is its own satisfaction. It's already complete.

All my life I have felt this longing. I guess it's how I travel in the world; it's what takes me where I'm going.

The longing for connection calls forth a life of connection. The longing that took me to the secret place in the bayberry bushes is the same longing that has taken me, as an adult, to spending months in a monastery; joining a voter registration drive; and setting the table for family and friends. My small self continues to reach for something beyond myself. The girl practicing handstands in that secret place is still with me, keeping me company. If that little kid can bear the longing, I can bear it. I remember that this is who I am, the one who wonders.

# Talking to My Dead Mother

WHEN MY EIGHTY-FOUR-YEAR-OLD mother was in the hospital after a car accident, I flew to Chicago to be with her. In my hasty departure, I took no other shoes but the ones on my feet, and they fell apart the day I got there, as I hurried across the hospital parking lot. The next day, oddly, a new pair of shoes arrived at my mother's apartment. She had ordered them for herself from a catalog. The black leather walking shoes fit me well; sturdy and comfortable, they were just what I needed. I told my mother that I was borrowing her new shoes until she got better, but she never did.

I've been wearing them almost daily ever since she died. I've taken them twice to my local shoe repair shop in Berkeley to have the Velcro fastenings replaced. I feel superstitious about them. I don't want them ever to wear out, but of course they will.

When my mother died, I became an orphan. At sixty-three, I was too old to feel like a waif, and yet I did. When I was a child, my friends and I played orphan games; we were playing, I now suppose, at what we feared the most. We were brave and strong. Shipwrecked without any parents on the desert island that was my back yard, we lived in imaginary tree houses, tamed palomino horses, made hammocks out of vines, gathered wild bananas and raspberries to eat—it was a great life. But being an orphan isn't like that at all; since my mother's death, I haven't done any of those things.

And, in a strange contradiction, the very event that turned me into an orphan also turned me into a matriarch. At my nephew's wedding, with our large extended family, I was the oldest person there. How could this have come to pass?

I'm the first of four siblings, and now both parents are gone, as well as all the aunts and uncles. The generations have rolled over: two months before my mother died, my granddaughter was born, the first of her generation in my family. For many years, the word *Grandma* was synonymous with my mother, who adored and was adored by her nine grandchildren. Yet I'm the grandma now. Everyone has to get up out of their chair and move over one notch. I'm sitting in my mother's seat, sometimes literally. I have her beloved "steamer chair" on my back porch, and I like sitting in it on warm days.

I'm also wearing some of my mother's clothes. When my sisters and I were going through her closet after her death, I took shirts and sweaters that would have been too Mother-Hubbardish for me before: a blue denim shirt, for example, with daisies embroidered on the bodice. Some impulse of loyalty to my mother makes me like it, and besides, it's comfy, and comfort trumps style these days. I also took a pair of black leather gloves, and a black wool jacket with brass buttons, made by Tibetan refugees. Sometimes, walking down the street in Berkeley on a chilly day, I look down to see that my body is embraced by my mother's coat, my mother's gloves, and my mother's shoes.

As an adolescent, I used to resent being closely identified with my mother. I went to the same small girls' high school that she had attended twenty years before me. Two of my teachers—an English teacher and a Latin teacher—sometimes called me by my mother's name, "Alice." In my senior year, I was glad to be chosen as the editor of the high school literary magazine, except that my mother had also had that job, and I was afraid that I might be under some kind of spell to live her life over again. But hadn't I come into the world to be a different person?

After high school, through various adventures and misadventures of my own, I clearly established that I was *not* my mother, and I stopped worrying about it. But now again my identity overlaps with my mother's. Sometimes people tell me I look like her, and now that she's gone I don't mind it as much as I used to. I'm not happy, though, about all the food stains I've been getting on my shirts, just as my mother did—spots of yogurt on the front and smears of chocolate ice cream on the cuffs.

It's strange how family likeness rises to the surface later in life, especially after a parent dies. My sisters, too, increasingly resemble my mother, and after my father died, my brother quite suddenly came to look startlingly like him. After my paternal grandmother died, my aunt took on my grandmother's face and form. She even seemed to foster the likeness, cutting her hair in a short gray wave as my grandmother had done and wearing what could have been the very same navy blue skirt and matching jacket my grandmother wore. Once, seeing her at a family gathering after an absence of a couple of years, I thought for a frightening moment that she *was* my dead grandmother. Perhaps our DNA is a time-release capsule, and at a certain stage the genes kick in to say: this is how the people in your family look when they get old.

I miss my mother more than I expected to. I'm also sad that she died because of an accident, before she was quite ready to go, and that her last three weeks were spent in the hospital, painfully encumbered by machinery that tried, and failed, to save her life. I want my sadness to be erased—for her to stop being dead, or for me to stop minding—but no such tidiness is likely to come while I'm alive.

And I'm finding out something surprising: even after my mother's death I still have a relationship with her, and it's a relationship that can change, even though she keeps on being dead. How I relate to her now is up to me.

I have a friend who used to take her father to a waterfront park in Berkeley and sit with him on a particular bench to look at the view. He died fifteen years ago, and she still goes there to sit on "Bubba's bench" and talk to him. After my mother died, I hung a photo of her in the stairwell of my house so that I meet her face to face every time I come downstairs. Sometimes I hear myself saying out loud, "Hi, Mom."

My mother had published several books of poetry with small presses, and at the end of her life, she wanted to publish a collection of her autobiographical short stories. She asked me to be her editor, which I was glad to do, so I helped her choose which of her stories to include, and I made suggestions as to how she might revise them. She also wrote some new stories for the collection. We had a good time working on this project together; I respected her writing and was moved by the life she told of in the stories, and she trusted my editorial responses.

A year before my mother's death, I took her to a writing workshop taught by an old friend, at Glenstal Abbey, a Benedictine abbey in the west of Ireland. It was our last big adventure together. There were only seven students: my mother and myself, four literary monks from the abbey, and a woman from Dublin. My mother worked on her last story there, about her painful marriage to my father, and she bravely read a piece of it aloud to the group each day when it was her turn. It was brave because the story told of intimate marital unhappiness, and the group included both celibate monks and her daughter. Everyone listened hard and gave her helpful feedback, and all that week she threw herself into her work, rewriting by hand because she didn't have a computer there, cutting and pasting with scissors and tape. One of the monks, with whom she fell quite in love, made photocopies for her in the library. It was a good story, and she made it better.

At mealtimes I pushed her in her wheelchair down the gravel

path to the refectory—it was slow going, crunching through the gravel—for blood pudding, brown bread, and tea in bowls with the monks. Evenings, in the late sunlight of the Irish summer, I took her to the walled garden, and she sat on the stone edge of the raised lavender bed and leaned into the smell.

The only moment of tension between us came one morning when my mother said, "I like your hair so much better when you brush it back." It was a familiar refrain, but this time I took it as a compliment, as I had just finished brushing my hair in the bathroom.

"Thank you," I said.

"No," she said, "not like that. Can't you just brush it back?" I was outraged, but later, looking at photos of myself on that trip, I saw that my hair was indeed unruly. I didn't cut my hair short and neat, getting it out of my face as she always wanted me to, until after her death. It must have been unconscious filial perversity that made me withhold this satisfaction from her. If she could only see my hair now, she would finally approve.

I was in her room in the abbey guesthouse when she received a call from an old man in Chicago who had shortly before become attentive to her. From across the room I could hear his voice at the other end of the line, on the other side of the Atlantic Ocean, shouting, "I love you!"

"Me, too," she said, too embarrassed in my presence to say the words back. She didn't know I'd heard his words, or that I was pleased by them, for her sake.

Soon after the trip to Ireland, my mother finished her revisions of all the stories, and it was left for me to do the final editing. I was making slow progress, because I was working on another editing project.

"When are you going to finish editing my book?" she asked me, every time we spoke.

"As soon as I finish this other project," I told her.

And then I did finish editing the other book, and I turned my full attention to my mother's book. I had just sent her my final edits when she was in the car accident that caused her death three weeks later.

I felt terrible that I hadn't finished the book in time for her to see it in print. But this is what happens when people die. Death interrupts life. Some process is going on, some piece of business, large or small, is unfinished, some words still unspoken, a letter unsent, a cup not yet washed, a shirt on the bed waiting to be folded.

I promised my mother in the hospital that I would finish the editing and publish the book, and so I did. When it came back from the printer, I opened the box with excitement and pulled out a copy, with a painting by a friend of my mother's on the cover. I held it, and it was perfect. My hands ached to complete the gesture—to put the book in my mother's hands.

I reassure myself that the pain of not finishing this project before she died is more mine than hers, for she had finished her work on the book, and she seemed to be focused on other concerns as she was dying: on her family and close friends, on breathing. Besides, putting the book together and getting it published gave me a way to work closely with my mother even after her death. She was a quieter collaborator than she had been when alive, but I continued to feel her presence as my siblings and I gave readings and sent the book out into the world, where people appreciated it.

My mother stopped taking care of her children in the ordinary sense long before she died; we have been grown-ups for a long time now. But she encouraged me and gave me comfort. She always wanted to hear from me, she always wanted to see me, and she admired whatever I did. As long as she was alive, I could keep on hoping that when I was having a hard time she could somehow make it better. Now that I'm an orphan I have to admit she isn't going to step in anymore.

I wish I had been better able to offer her comfort in return. She didn't ask for it often, but it was hard for me to listen to her when she was unhappy about something. As the mother, she was the one who was supposed to comfort me. I jumped too quickly to "Oh, it couldn't be that bad, I'm sure he didn't mean to hurt your feelings," and this made matters worse because she felt dismissed.

As I experience some of what my mother went through when she grew old, I sympathize with her in a new way. I realize in retrospect how little she complained, in spite of serious problems like the disabling pain in her back that limited her walking. Paradoxically, she got tougher as she got frailer.

But she did complain that I didn't visit her enough. I used to go to Chicago to see her a couple of times a year, for about a week each time. My stepfather died two years before my mother, and after his death it was more intimate, visiting her. I felt some awkwardness as the two of us sat in her living room, and I crocheted, and she stroked her cat, or tapped her forefinger against her upper lip, hoping for confidences from me that I didn't offer—how I felt about my life and the people in it. She didn't ask, but I could feel her wondering: *Did I have a lover? What was I writing about?* Damn! How hard would it have been to let down my guard? But I was relieved when it was 10:00 P.M., and we could turn on the BBC news, as was her habit. "I don't need to watch the news while you're visiting," she'd say. "I can watch the news any night."

"Oh, that's OK," I answered. "Let's find out about those forest fires in California."

My fear that my mother's needs would become too great for me made me keep a certain distance from her, out of a misguided self-protection. Now that she's dead, I have more distance than I want.

I used to call her every Sunday. We chatted about the weather, what we were reading, movies, news of her grandchildren, and she would tell me what she was seeing out of her sixth-floor window overlooking Lake Michigan. "Men in yellow hats are spreading sand, making a beach at the edge of the lake—they look like yellow ants." Or, "There's a fat woman jogging along the lake—I can't understand why such a fat person would ever go jogging. It's ridiculous!" One time she told me with great enthusiasm about the newly elected senator from Illinois who came from Hyde Park, her neighborhood of Chicago—Barack Obama.

A few years before she died, I started telling her I loved her, the last thing before I hung up the phone. I was over sixty and she was over eighty—an old daughter telling an old mother a simple thing that she was glad to hear. It was true, so I don't know why it was hard to say when I first began the practice, but it got easier as I got into the habit, and in the last couple of years it rolled right off my tongue.

Lots of things have happened that I would tell my mother about if I could call her next Sunday. I'd like her to know that people are crazy about her book of short stories. I'd like her to know that her great-granddaughter can talk in both English and Spanish. She would have loved to be at my nephew's wedding last summer, with the extended family all around. And she would be thrilled about Obama. I wish I could tell her—"Guess who's your president!"

The more time that goes by, the more events she'll miss: graduations and weddings and births, and she'll slip further into the past, and her grandchildren will marry people she never met, and take up interests she never knew they had, and her children will get old and feeble, and have joints replaced and troublesome organs removed.

I can appreciate my mother more now that I'm not reacting defensively to her criticisms of my unruly hair or feeling guilty that I'm not visiting her enough. As long as she was alive, she was Mom, and I, being her child no matter my age, became childish.

She birthed me twice: the first time when I was born, and the second when she died. Now that she's gone, there's no person on earth whose child I am. So I have to grow up, at this late date. It takes so long to grow up.

A year after my mother died, I was sitting in my parked car in the California countryside. My cell phone rang on the seat beside me. I fumbled for it and barely managed to answer it in time. "Hello?"

"Hello, it's *your mother*." That's how she always identified herself when she telephoned me, saying the words "your mother" with ironic emphasis, as if it was our private joke. Nobody ever reaches me on my cell phone, not even the living, because I never leave it on, so this was truly a miracle.

"Mom!" I said, overjoyed to hear her voice, "how wonderful that you've found a way to reach me even though you're dead! Thank you so much for calling."

"Please take good care of yourself, Susan," she said with affection. That was all, but when she said it, I knew it was exactly what I wanted to hear. Then I lost the connection.

It was enough. I was overcome with gratitude that she had contacted me from the other side. And when I woke up and realized it was just a dream, it was *still* a miracle. She had found a way to reach me.

# For the Time Being

The self is time . . . Do not think that time merely flies
away . . . If time merely flies away, you would be separated
from time.

—*Zen Master Dogen, "The Time Being"*

WHEN I WAS FORTY-NINE and my sons were more or less
grown, I kept a promise I had made to myself to go on a long
retreat before I turned fifty. I arranged a leave of absence from
my job, had a set of robes sewn for me, and went to a "practice
period" at Tassajara Zen Mountain Center, deep in the coastal
mountains of California. For three months I followed the strict
monastic schedule: meditating, studying Buddhist teachings, and
working in silence at whatever I was assigned to, whether it was
chopping carrots or cleaning kerosene lanterns. I didn't get in a
car or hear a phone ring the whole time.

Zen monks are called to zazen by the striking of the *han*, a
heavy wooden block that hangs from a rope beside the temple
entrance. The han is hit with a wooden mallet in an intricate
pattern that lasts for fifteen minutes, and at Tassajara, where the
monks' cabins stretch out along a narrow valley, a second han,
known as the echo han, hangs partway down the path, to pass the

signal along. You can tell how much time you have left to get to your cushion in the zendo by listening to the pattern.

The crack of wood on wood runs fast through the valley. Written in calligraphy on the block itself are the words:

Wake up!
Life is transient
swiftly passing
Be aware
The great matter
Don't waste
Time

One evening somewhere in the middle of the practice period, it was my turn to hit the echo han, strike for strike. I stood on the dusty path, mallet in hand, like a frog on a lily pad waiting for a fly. I faced the garden, where the evening sun came through a gap in the mountains and landed on a pair of apricot trees. I was poised in the brief interval between hits, waiting, and the weeks of the practice period stretched out before me and behind me into infinity. And when that next hit came to my ears, my arm lifted the mallet and whacked the board, no holding back, and then it was quiet, and the light was still on the apricot trees, and I was ready for the next one.

A couple of years ago, when I was a few months shy of being sixty-five, I packed up my things at work. I loved my job—I had loved it for seventeen years. But editing a magazine with a quarterly deadline meant that I was under constant time pressure. I wanted to retire before they had to gently push me out, before my brain wizened up right there at my desk, with the phone in one hand and the mouse in the other. I wanted to have time for other things before I died—quiet time, deep time—for writing, dharma, family and friends, and for something new and unknown.

———

The part of me that wants to lower my bucket into a deep well and draw up cool water is sabotaged by another part. I suffer from a condition that a Zen friend calls "FOMS Syndrome"—fear of missing something. It's a form of greed—the urge to cram as many interesting activities into the day as possible, coupled with the impulse to say yes to everything. To put it more positively, I'm curious about everything and everybody. And so, when I first retired, feeling rich with time, I signed up for all sorts of activities, classes, and projects. Each separate thing I was doing was worthwhile; I loved my Spanish class and my photography class, for example. But soon I was busier than before. Where was my deep time?

When I get too busy, old habits of mind kick in. I try to solve the problem by readjusting my schedule, which only makes it worse. I change one appointment in order to make room for another. I stare at my week-at-a glance calendar looking for white space, and when I find it, I pounce. Ah, a delicious piece of time! I write down: "2 pm—Nomad Café, plan workshop w. Jean," and the white space is gone. Woops! No more time. Then I feel like an animal flailing around in a trap made of netting, getting more tightly bound.

I try to measure out my time in the long run as well as the short. I'm a person who likes to count things, and I run the numbers. At sixty-six, I figure I'm about three-quarters of the way through. That's if I make it to eighty-eight. How long is that? I go backward twenty-two years, to when I was studying Russian and I went on a "citizen diplomacy" trip to the Soviet Union. Remember the Soviet Union? So I guess twenty-two years is a pretty long time—but it's all gone now, including my Russian. The next twenty-two years will go faster than the last, and besides, I might die sooner.

Like my father, who died at seventy-three. That would mean I've already lived—wait, let me check my calculator—90 percent of my life.

Admittedly, sometimes it's appropriate to think about time this way—to consult the actuarial tables of the mind. I have a seventy-year-old friend who has heart trouble and other chronic health problems. She's financially stressed, and she has to make decisions about her house and her living expenses. She has to decide how soon she can max out her equity line of credit, or whether she needs to keep on working part-time. She came right out and asked her cardiologist to give her a rough estimate of her life expectancy. She told him that she had tentatively figured out financing that would get her to the age of eighty-two.

"You've been doing well for the last few years," he told her. "According to the statistics, you have a better than fifty percent chance of living to the age of eighty-seven."

My friend rolled her eyes. "But I can't afford to live that long!" They both laughed, and now she's looking for more part-time work.

Of course you can't really measure time at all. Our calibrations are like pencil marks on the ocean. Einstein taught us that time is flexible. It passes differently for a person in commuter traffic, a person centering a lump of wet clay on a potter's wheel, or, so Einstein told us, a person approaching the speed of light in a spaceship. An hour can seem like a year and a year like an hour. In the last days of my father's dying, he was in a lot of pain from cancer. He would often ask what time it was, and whatever the answer was, he would groan and say, "Oh, no! Is that all it is?" I couldn't understand why he wanted time to hurry up, because there wasn't anything that was going to happen, except that he was going to die. I think the pain made time pass slowly, and he wanted to know that he was getting through it, from one hour to the next.

I, too, have had times when I wanted time to hurry by. Mostly, though, time is what I want more of, and as I get older, it gets scarcer and scarcer. First of all, there's less of it in front of me than there used to be. Second, each year swings by faster than the one before. Third, I'm no good at multitasking anymore—I can only do one thing at a time. And fourth, it takes me longer to do each thing. Age is forcing me to slow down.

I'm not the only one. There's got to be some biological reason that old people drive so slowly on the freeway. I just saw a bumper sticker that said: "Old and Slow."

I remember impatiently watching my grandmother making peanut butter and jelly sandwiches for a picnic. She got the jam out of the cupboard and put it on the blue linoleum countertop, and then she walked back across the kitchen to the same cupboard for the peanut butter. It took forever. Well, not quite forever, because she did make the sandwiches, and we ate them on a plaid blanket down in the meadow.

Here's the amazing thing: aging is giving me back the present moment. It's only linear time that's shrinking, and as it does, I have a better chance to enter deep time. It only takes a few seconds to slip through the crack between two hits of the han into a timeless garden.

This is what zazen is all about: it's time out of time, it's stepping aside from activity and slowing down to a full stop. While I'm sitting zazen, even if my monkey mind is swinging wildly from branch to branch, at least I'm not accomplishing anything useful. As the Heart Sutra says, "There is no attainment, with nothing to attain."

It's easy to get nothing done while sitting zazen; a person of any age can do it. But now that I'm getting older, I'm learning to accomplish practically nothing in the rest of my day as well. If the trend continues, my next-door neighbor will think I'm doing standing meditation in the back yard when I'm actually taking in the laundry.

I like to bury my face in the sunny smell of the sheet on the line before I take it down. I like the slow squeak of the line through the rusty pulley as I haul in another sweet pillowcase. The laundry lines of my childhood made exactly that noise.

I'm not saying I'm ready to quit. In spite of what the *Heart Sutra* tells me, I still have things I want to accomplish in the world beyond the laundry line; and then I want to go on to something new, something I can do with other people to help this feverish planet. I want to keep working—I use the word *working* broadly. I'm learning that slowing down is the way. I have to pay attention to my natural rhythms. I try to let each thing take as long as it takes, and I'm putting some white space back into my appointment calendar. I've made a rule for myself that I mostly keep: no appointments, no telephone calls, and no e-mail before noon. Mornings are for writing and study; I can look at the to-do list in the afternoon.

Now layers of time live in me. I think of this layering as vertical time, when all time flows into the present moment, as opposed to the horizontal time lines that used to appear on classroom wall charts: on the left, the beginning of bipedal human life when our ancestors came down from the trees four million years ago in the Pliocene epoch, and then, at the other end of the long line, the current Holocene epoch, in which we hominids can travel via the Internet to look down at the melting polar ice cap without ever getting up from our chairs. It's all in me, in the present moment. Even though I don't have a clear recollection of our Pliocene days, this body remembers how it feels to climb down from a tree, swinging by your arms from the lowest bough, then letting go of the rough bark in your hands and dropping to solid earth like a ball into a catcher's glove.

When old people get the generations mixed up and call a grandson by a brother's name, they're not wrong. They're living in the deep time that Dogen calls the "time being." "Each moment is all being, is the entire world. Reflect now whether any being or any world is left out of the present moment."

I think of time as the landscape I'm traveling through on a train, and the train is my life. I can only see what's outside the window. Yesterday was Naperville, Illinois; today is Grand Junction, Colorado; tomorrow will be Sparks, Nevada. I just see the piece that's framed by the train window, but it's all there at once, all those places, the whole continent.

I was visiting my granddaughter Paloma on her third birthday; we went to the neighborhood swimming pool and played in the shallow end, and she poured pailfuls of water over my head, pretending she was washing my hair. She looks like her father when he was a small child, when I sat on the closed toilet lid in the bathroom while he took his bath, watching him fill graduated plastic cups with water and line them up along the edge of the bathtub for Snow White and Peter Pan to swim in. My three-year-old self was with Paloma, too, on another hot summer day, filling a wooden bucket from the hand pump in my grandmother's garden in order to "paint" the garden chairs. Playing in the pool with Paloma, I didn't think of those watery long-ago moments consciously; I didn't need to. As Paloma turned her bucket upside down over my head, *long ago* disappeared, and those other childhoods, those other summers, flowed over me and soaked my skin.

Before we left the pool, Paloma went over to the lifeguard sitting in his elevated chair; she held up three fingers and called, "Hi, Lifeguard! I'm three! I'm three!" Threeness was in me, too. I can't be in more than one place at the same time, but I can be in more than one time in the same place.

Time is not something I have; it's what I'm made of.

# Alone with Everyone

THROUGHOUT MY LIFE I've struggled with loneliness and the fear of loneliness. Through my Buddhist practice I've gradually come to understand that I'm not alone, even when I'm alone, at least in theory.

I was past sixty when a sabbatical from work gave me the opportunity, and I finally felt ready to turn theory into practice. I decided to spend a month alone in the woods—in a small hippie-style hand-built cabin on a piece of land I own with two other families in Mendocino County. I've been going up there for twenty-five years. It's a great place to go with someone you love, but I've never liked going there alone because it's so isolated, and I've been afraid to get out on that lonesome limb. But now I felt ready. I wanted to find out who was there when there was nobody there but me.

How do you really know you're alive, that you're a person, if there's nobody around to say, "Yeah! I know what you mean!" Or even, "Hey! You stepped on my toe!" So this was the core question I had. If a tree falls in the forest, and nobody hears it . . . ? If a woman sits on a porch in the woods, and nobody sees her . . . ?

The cabin is two miles up a steep dirt road on a ridge. There's no electricity, no phone, no cell phone access, no refrigeration. There's a wood stove for heat and a propane stove for cooking. The outhouse boasts an excellent view. The nearest neighbor lives half a mile up the road and works in the town of Willits, a half hour's drive away.

It was my intention not to see or speak to anyone for a whole month. How often do you go even one day without seeing or speaking to another person? It practically never happens. Some people in my life couldn't understand what I was up to. My mother's initial response was, "What would you want to do that for?" And even in Soto Zen practice, we don't have a tradition of solitary retreat, as there is in Tibetan Buddhism.

I planned the experience carefully. I arranged with the neighbor up the road to drop off some fresh produce twice during the month, but mostly I ate oatmeal, rice and beans, beets and potatoes. I also arranged with my dharma friend and mentor Norman Fischer to be my contact person. Once a week, to keep myself from feeling totally isolated, and so that my family would know I hadn't been killed by a mountain lion, I would drive twenty minutes down the road and call Norman from a pay phone at a rest stop on Highway 101. That was to be the only time I would use my car and the only time I would talk to another human being.

My sister kindly let me borrow her gentle long-legged dog, Satchmo, to keep me company. He looks like a deer, especially when he leaps up the hillside through the manzanita bushes. I wanted him with me because a bear had been hanging around the cabin for a year or so; it had broken in several times and trashed all the food, and once my son had encountered it on his way to the outhouse in the middle of the night. He told me he shined his flashlight straight into its eyes and it turned and ambled away, but I couldn't picture myself doing that. I was scared of this bear, even though it's not the kind of bear that eats people. I thought Satchmo would make me feel more secure—and he did. More important, he provided tender, limbic companionship. We were in constant communication. But I still had to grapple with being the only English-speaking creature around.

I didn't take a watch, because I wanted to explore time in a new way. I wanted to be in the present moment as much as possible. I was taking a break from my week-at-a-glance calendar, from a life of rushing from one appointment to the next, worrying about being late. I wanted to have the experience of getting up when I woke up, eating when I was hungry, and going to bed when I was sleepy. I didn't want to know what time it was by the clock.

I developed a routine. I got up and took Satchmo for a walk. Then I meditated for the length of a stick of incense. I had breakfast, and spent the morning reading and writing. I had brought my laptop with me, along with a little gizmo to recharge it off the car battery by plugging it into the cigarette lighter.

When my belly told me it was lunchtime I ate lunch, and in the afternoons I did some kind of work project. I found myself surprisingly excited about sawing boards, building a bookcase, clearing trails, fixing benches, stacking firewood. After tiring myself out, I would sit down on the cabin porch and drink a cup of black tea with honey and powdered milk in it.

This porch was the bridge of my ship, from which I steered my way through that September, looking across a valley to the layers of mountains on the other side. The weather was perfect for my voyage: warm in the day but not too hot, and cool at night but not cold. After my tea, Satchmo and I would go for our afternoon walk.

In the late afternoon, I'd return to my perch on the porch and read, and when it got too dark for my rods and cones to see the words, I'd go inside and meditate for the length of another stick of incense. And then I'd have supper.

But after supper I didn't know what to do. Sometimes I read or crocheted, or tried to teach myself the ukulele. I had various projects lined up. But actually, I found that the kerosene lanterns just didn't have the vigor to get me up to anything very challenging. I faded in the evening. It was dark, and there were strange sounds—scratching on the roof, or Satchmo growling at something. And so I would go to bed.

I was taking care of myself. I was collecting kindling and cutting firewood to be ready in case it got cold. I had to fix the water line one time when there was a leak from the water tank, and I was proud of myself for figuring out how to do it. I was cooking three meals a day for myself, because I was eating the kind of food you have to prepare, so when I made a delicious black lentil stew for myself I figured, "There must be somebody here, otherwise why would I be making all this black lentil stew for her?" I'm a person. I need to stay warm. I need to get water. I need to eat. I'm accustomed to taking care of other people, but taking care of myself turned out to be a satisfying project, too, as if an exchange student, who happened to be me, had come to live with me for a month. I saw that she deserved to be taken care of, maybe even for more than a month.

The hardest times for me were each day at twilight. Ever since I was a child, I've gotten lonesome at twilight. There's something about that in-between time when it's not day anymore but it's not yet night. The day was on its deathbed—I watched it lie down on the brown hills. And up there, alone, what I call twilight sickness came over me. Why was I all alone? It was out of my control; the feeling just came like an uninvited guest. It varied in intensity but there was always a taste of grief at the end of the day.

The insects sang out—katydids? crickets?—farewell, day; hello, night. I tried to catch the moment when they started their klezmer song but I always missed it. When I first heard them, they were already singing, like the first star, always already shining. I had no one to be at my side "at the end of the day," as they say.

I could have tried to distract myself from the twilight sickness, could have cranked up my wind-up radio and listened to KMUD in Garberville, where countercultural country folk were always bashing Bush and so providing a certain amount of company. But the wind-up radio ran down—it was only a stopgap measure.

So I sat down on my round black cushion in the loft to face the twilight. I vowed to sit there until it was night. Through the tall window, I watched the day give up the ghost. Where the sky met the line of the Yolla Bolly Mountains, I saw a color with no name, between green and pink. I slipped down in the loss of light, and my own life seemed to fade with the day—all I loved was gone; all I'd done was wrong. The dark ate the trees, leaf by leaf.

And still I sat there, staring down my mind. I had come by choice to be alone on Shimmins Ridge, like a monk in a Chinese scroll. "What is it?" I shouted. "What is it?"

At last, twilight was gone. I went down the steep stairs and lit the lamps and ate my rice and beans in a time that was no longer in between, a time that was simply night.

Evening after evening, I sat there with my demons, asking: What is it? Finally, I saw that it was nothing. It was OK. I began to believe that I was sitting in the lap of Buddha.

As the quiet days went by and I opened to my surroundings, nature helped me understand that I was not alone. Bats, quail, woodpeckers, deer. When the crickets are singing and the leaves are whispering, you feel the vibrations of all the life that's passing through you. Even the rattlesnake curled up on the outdoor shower platform in the sun provided a certain amount of company as it rattled at me before slithering away into the woodpile.

One afternoon I was on the porch doing some yoga. I was feeling good and strong and enjoying myself, but noisy planes kept roaring overhead. I love the silence of that place, and I was annoyed by the unusual disturbance. When I finally looked up and paid attention, I saw that there were huge billows of smoke wafting toward me from the valley below. I realized with a shock that there was a forest fire nearby, and these were forestry planes. I couldn't tell where the fire was because of the trees, but it looked like the smoke could be coming from the little valley right at the bottom of our dirt road. I got anxious. If the fire was down on Covelo Road, it could tear its way up through the dry trees on the ridge in a flash, and Satchmo and I would be done for. So we got into the car to drive down the hill and check it out. But the car wouldn't start—the battery was dead! If only I had parked the car at the top of the slope I could have put it in second gear and rolled down till the engine caught, but I'd tucked the car into a parking spot off the road.

I had a bad moment then. I thought about the Oakland fire, and the people who died because they couldn't get down from the Oakland Hills. I thought: my family and friends will be so annoyed with me if I burn to death because I drained my car battery with my laptop!

I knew my uphill neighbor was at work in town, so Satchmo and I walked to the next-nearest neighbor's house a mile down the road, but he wasn't there. I was probably the only living person on Shimmins Ridge. We walked another mile down to the bottom of our dirt road, and by that time I could tell by the smoke that the fire was on the other side of another ridge. What a relief! Down at the bottom, on the paved road, I found some neighbors at home—in the country, people two miles away are neighbors—and the other neighbors on my dirt road who hadn't been home were there, too, and they were all sitting around drinking beer on a weekday afternoon.

They told me not to worry about the fire—they had gone online and found out it was across the highway. I said I had a dead battery, and one of the guys offered to drive me up the hill in his truck and give me a jump start. Then they gave me a glass of water, and we chatted for about half an hour, and nobody did anything about giving me a ride. I didn't say, "When are you going to give me a jump start?" I wasn't in any hurry. It seemed that nobody was. More hummingbirds than I have ever seen at once were buzzing around a dozen feeders, and I watched them. I hadn't talked to anybody for two weeks, so I was in some kind of altered state anyway. I was content to wait. But I was struck by the fact that if somebody back in the city, back in Berkeley, said they'd give you a jump start, they wouldn't just keep sitting there for another half an hour as if they hadn't said it. Finally the guy said, "OK, let's go," and he drove me and Satchmo up the road in his pickup truck, and started my car.

It was a humbling experience. I had been feeling so proud of myself for being a pioneer woman taking care of herself in the wilderness. I had been annoyed with the planes—those manifestations of technological pollution. Then suddenly everything flipped, and I realized that even there, on retreat in the woods, I was completely woven into the tapestry of human society. I was grateful that the Forestry Department had planes to put out forest fires and that there were friendly people at the bottom of the road who could give me a jump start, and I saw that my whole retreat was resting on a foundation of human goodwill and human society.

Near the end of my sojourn, I had a severe relapse of loneliness. As it happened, I left the cabin for a day and a half to go to the memorial service of a dear family friend. I took Satchmo back to my sister's in Berkeley and joined with people I love to celebrate the long life of a man who had devoted himself to art and family. Afterward, I drove north again, dogless, for the final week of my retreat.

When I got back to the cabin that evening, I fell apart. I was by myself again, without even Satchmo to keep me company. It was twilight, and I'd forgotten what I was doing there. I compared my life to my deceased friend's—he had always made art, always loved and lived with family. All my worst fears and all my regrets about being alone flamed up again, and I thought I might not be able to last the week. I sat in meditation, and I cried.

The next morning, still crying, I walked, I meditated, I made lentil soup, and I cleared some brush. As I sat in the twilight that evening, looking out at the oak tree shining in the last light,

I reminded myself of what Norman had said in our last phone conversation. It's natural to feel sadness at the ending of the day, and it's natural to feel sadness on parting from loved ones. Impermanence is sad, but when I beat myself up with regret, I'm robbing myself of the life I'm living right now: the Spanish moss on the oak branch, the crickets' chant, the smell of lentil soup on the stove. I felt . . . a shift, a lift, a clicking into place. In the next couple of days, my loneliness fever broke, and I returned to myself again.

One morning as I was returning from a long walk, I looked up and there was the gibbous moon, just past full and nibbled along one side by the passage of time, floating in the bright blue sky above some digger pines. It was suddenly the most beautiful thing I'd ever seen. I felt as though the moon was having a party and had invited me to come.

I believe now that I'm OK in a way I didn't believe it before. Now, when the twilight sickness comes again, as it surely will, I hope I'll know, even in that sadness, that I'm alone with everyone.

# This Vast Life

Every morning, I vow to be grateful for the precious gift of human birth. It's a big gift, and it includes a lot of stuff I never particularly wanted for my birthday. Some of the things in the package I wish I could exchange for a different size or color. But I want to find out what it means to be a human being—my curiosity remains intense even as I get older—so I say thanks for the whole thing. It's all of a piece.

In thirteenth-century Japan, Zen Master Dogen wrote, "The Way is basically perfect and all-pervading." I'm already in it. We are all in it; we are made of it.

When my granddaughter was just over two, I visited her and her parents in Texas. She doesn't have a lot of ideas yet about how things are supposed to be, or what's supposed to happen next. She's glad to be alive. I was babysitting for her one afternoon, and part of my job was to get her up from her nap. I was reading in the next room, and I knew when she woke up because I heard her chatting away to her bear. I lifted her and her bear out of her crib and we went downstairs. While I fixed her a snack of crackers and cheese, she danced around a purple ball that was lying in the middle of the living room, singing an old nursery rhyme that she had learned in her preschool: "Ring around the rosies, pocket full of posies, ashes, ashes, we all fall down." And then she sat down on the floor—*kerplunk!*—laughing. She was fully present, fully joyful. Actually, the song she was singing is a very old chant about the plague, and the last line about the ashes refers to our mortality. But she wasn't worrying about that.

In his poetic essay "The Genjokoan," Master Dogen wrote, "A fish swims in the ocean, and no matter how far it swims, there is no end to the water. A bird flies in the sky, and no matter how far it flies, there is no end to the air."

When I get unhappy about something in my life, I think: "Wait, no, this isn't the right life, it isn't what I want, I need to find the edge of this life and leap over the fence into a different life." But that's not how it works. My life is vast. I can't find the edge of it, just like a fish in the ocean or a bird in the sky. There's no getting out of this life, this ocean, this sky, except by dying. If I try to change oceans, I'll never find my way or my place—there's no place else to be but here, in the big mystery of it.

It happened that only a few days after visiting my grand-daughter I visited an old friend in his eighties who lives in an assisted living facility. He's a Catholic priest and monk who has dedicated his life to solitude and spiritual study. He's well read in multiple spiritual traditions, including Zen, and he is an important mentor to me. For many years he has been leading me in an ongoing conversation about prayer, mysticism, and spiritual inquiry, through correspondence as well as face-to-face visits.

He's not well physically, he's weak, on oxygen, and confined to a wheelchair, but his mind is fine.

He told me, "If I've died before, I don't remember it, but I recognize what's happening—that's where I'm going." Years ago he had a coffin built for himself by a carpenter he knows. It stands upright in his little apartment like a roommate, a reminder, keeping him company. He sits at his table and looks out the window at a pear tree, and watches its leaves turn, and fall, and bud again. He watches the seasons, the whole universe, in that pear tree. He reads, he prays, he receives an occasional visitor. Like my granddaughter, he is completely present in his life. Like Dogen's fish, he is swimming around in his ocean, and there is no end to the water, even in this tiny apartment.

Moments after I entered his room he was talking to me about Isaac of Ninevah, the eighth-century Syrian hermit, whose writings he had been reading when I came in.

Like my granddaughter, he, too, is singing his version of ring around the rosies, dancing until he falls down and turns to ashes.

In between that toddler and that old man is a span of over eighty years—and most of us, in those intervening decades, tangle ourselves up in knots over the things we don't have that we want, and the things we have that we don't want. We run around trying to fix things, in our personal lives and in the life of the planet. It's a good thing we do, because it's actually our responsibility to fix things; we need to fix the plumbing, for example. The toddler and the old monk aren't fixing the plumbing. They need us to take care of them, but we need them, too, to remind us that everything is already taken care of.

I like to think about how we are completely held by the atmosphere in a literal way. The air that surrounds each of our bodies, that flows in and out of our lungs, is not nothing. It's thick with molecules, and it fills up all the gaps and cracks between us and the other bodies and objects around us: the furniture, the walls of the room, the trees outside, the buildings. There's no empty space. The air is fluid, making room for us, so that each of us inhabits a nook that is exactly our size and shape. The air kindly moves with us when we move. It's like those soft rocks you can find on the beaches of northern California that have tiny mollusks living inside them in the holes they made for themselves. We're all connected, molecule to molecule. I'm held by everything that's not me.

———

The last meditation retreat I attended was beside the ocean, and while I was sitting I listened to the surf. The surf is the sound of the ocean breathing. It's never still. Sometimes the sea is so loud and crashing that I crave a little silence, and so I listen for the silence between the waves, but just as one wave recedes from the shore, flowing back down the sand into the ocean, getting quieter and quieter, just before it gets silent, the next wave always breaks. The ocean never stops breathing because it's alive. As I sit on my seat in the zendo, following my breathing, I follow the breathing of the ocean, too, and I begin to breathe in rhythm with the ocean.

The sound of the ocean is the sound of time passing, the sound of one moment giving way to the next. Each wave, each moment, is a gate that I pass through into the next moment.

And even if I'm not sitting by the ocean, one wave of my life is still followed immediately by the next, with no completely quiet place in between.

I love the vow: "Dharma gates are boundless; I vow to enter them." I keep giving myself away to the next moment, and the next moment receives me. I just have to step through.

# Acknowledgments

I AM GRATEFUL to my editors at Shambhala Publications: to Dave O'Neal, who encouraged me to write the book in the first place, and to Emily Bower, whose skillful and supportive responses have helped me give it shape.

Many thanks to Ellery Akers, Sarah Balcomb, Mary Barrett, Andrew Boyd, Susan Butler, Louise Dunlap, Barbara Gates, Fanny Howe, Bonnie O'Brien Jonsson, Linda Norton, Susan Orr, Bob Perelman, Nora Ryerson, Prue See, Barbara Selfridge, Gail Seneca, Francie Shaw, and Jeff Sharlet for their editorial suggestions. Thanks to the members of my Crones Group, Melody Ermachild Chavis, Annette Herskovits, Cheeta Llanes, and Judith Tannenbaum, for thinking and talking with me in a focused way about getting old, and to all my other friends and relatives who have been part of that ongoing conversation. Thanks to Blue Mountain Center, Glenstal Abbey, and the Berkeley Public Library for giving me beautiful places to work.

# Credits and Permissions

The poem on page 67 by Izumi Shikibu, translated by Jane Hirshfield and Mariko Aratani, is from *Women in Praise of the Sacred* (p. 59), edited by Jane Hirshfield, copyright ©1994 by Jane Hirshfield, reprinted by permission of HarperCollins Publishers.

The poem on page 68 is reprinted from *The First Buddhist Women: Translations and Commentary on the Therigatha*, p. 59, (1991) by Susan Murcott, with permission of Parallax Press, Berkeley, California. www.parallax.org

The haiku on page 137 is from *One Robe, One Bowl: The Zen Poetry of Ryōkan*, translated and introduced by John Stevens, First edition, 1977. Protected by copyright under the terms of the International Copyright Union. Reprinted by arrangement with Shambhala Publications Inc., Boston, MA. www.shambhala .com.

The quotations from Dogen on pages x, 7, 153, and 169 are from *Moon in a Dewdrop*, ed. Kazuaki Tanahashi (San Francisco: Northpoint Press, 1985).

The quotations from Robert Aitken and Alice Hayes on pages xi–xii are both from the Winter 2001 issue of *Turning Wheel* (p. 21).

The quotations on pages 21 and 68 are both from Dogen's "Fukanzazengi" in *The Heart of Dogen's Shobogenzo*, trans. Masao Abe and Norman Waddell (Albany: State University of New York Press, 2002).

The quotation from May Sarton on page 68 is from "Rewards of a Solitary Life," *New York Times*, 1990.

Verse on page 70 is from Shantideva, *The Way of the Bodhisattva*, trans. Padmakara Translation Group (Shambhala Publications, 2006), verse 120, p. 126.

The story on page 97 about Dogen's student is told by Taisen Deshimaru in "With Grandmother's Mind," published on the website of the New Orleans Zen Temple, www.nozt.org, and originally published in Deshimaru's book, *Le Bol et le Baton* (Paris: Albin Michel, 1986).

The quotation from the Prajna Paramita Sutra on page 130 is from *The Perfection of Wisdom in Eight Thousand Lines*, translated by Edward Conze (Portland, Maine: Four Seasons, 1973), p.135.